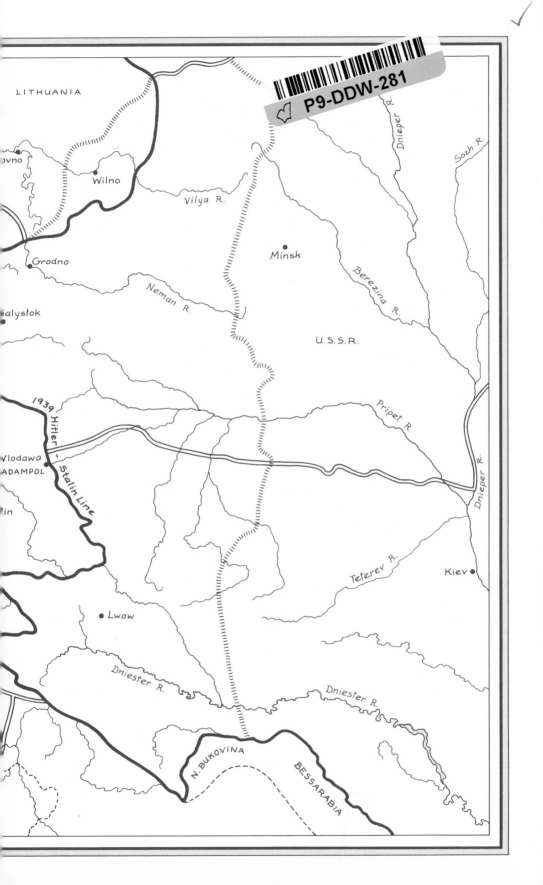

LITHUANIA

ovno

Wilno

Vilya R.

Dnieper R.

Sozh R.

P9-DDW-281

Grodno

Minsk

Berezina R.

ialystok

Neman R.

U.S.S.R.

1939 Hitler –

Wlodawa
ADAMPOL

Stalin Line

Pripet R.

Dnieper R.

lin

Teterev R.

Kiev

Lwow

Dniester R.

Dniester R.

N. BUKOVINA

BESSARABIA

Have You Forgotten?

HAVE YOU FORGOTTEN?

a memoir of Poland 1939–1945

BY *CHRISTINE ZAMOYSKA-PANEK*

WITH *Fred Benton Holmberg*

DOUBLEDAY

NEWYORK • LONDON • TORONTO • SYDNEY • AUCKLAND

PUBLISHED BY DOUBLEDAY
a division of Bantam Doubleday Dell Publishing Group, Inc.
666 Fifth Avenue, New York, New York 10103

Doubleday and the portrayal of an anchor with a dolphin
are trademarks of Doubleday, a division of
Bantam Doubleday Dell Publishing Group, Inc.

Library of Congress Cataloging-in-Publication Data
Zamoyska-Panek, Christine.
Have you forgotten? : a memoir of Poland, 1939–1945 / by Christine
Zamoyska-Panek with Fred Benton Holmberg.—1st ed.
p. cm.
1. Zamoyska-Panek, Christine.   2. World War, 1939–1945—
Underground movements—Poland.   3. World War, 1939–1945—Personal
narratives, Polish.   4. Guerrillas—Poland—Biography.   5. Poland—
Nobility—Biography.   I. Holmberg, Fred Benton.   II. Title.
D802.P6Z33   1989
940.53′438—dc20
89-31965
CIP

Book Design by Guenet Abraham

September 1989
FIRST EDITION

BG

Have you forgotten yet? . . .
Look down, and swear by the slain of the War that you'll never forget.

"Aftermath"
Siegfried Sassoon
March 1919

TO MY DEAR LATE HUSBAND J.P., WHOSE SPIRIT HAS ALWAYS
BEEN MY GUIDING LIGHT

$\sim\cdot$ *FOREWORD* $\cdot\backsim$

Have You Forgotten? is a story commemorating the fiftieth anniversary of the Germàn and Russian invasion of Poland. Although it is an autobiography, it is the story of many determined people who joined bravely together, defending human rights, and who, as a nation, never bowed to its enemies.

I carry in my heart deep gratitude to all my friends and family for helping me to survive the many dangers encountered during World War II. It was the closeness of our family that gave us all the strength to endure in those days.

My gratitude extends to Fred and Diane Holmberg, who helped to compile this material and to record it in book form. I thank my editor, Jacqueline Kennedy Onassis, for her sensitivity in understanding and helping me to publish this story. My appreciation to Iwo Cyprian Pogonowski, whose maps were the basis for the ones used in this book.

Finally I thank all of my friends, who a long time ago encouraged me to write down my memories.

My project would never have been realized without the support I received from my mother; Jerome, my brother; Andrew, my cousin; and my friends Stanton and Susie Deland, Hilda Rothschild, Maryann Shelley, and Margareta Lindstrom.

∾ · *THE FAMILY OF CHRISTINE ZAMOYSKA* · ∽

MAMA ·	Countess Nathalie Lubomirska Zamoyska ·	*Mother*
TATEK ·	Count Constantine Zamoyski ·	*Father*
DZIADZIO ·	Prince Stefan Lubomirski ·	*Grandfather*
BABCIA ·	Princess Natalia Lubomirska ·	*Grandmother*
BUNIA ·	Countess Rose Zamoyska ·	*Grandmother*
JEROME ·	The Young Count ·	*Brother*
BASIA ·	The Young Countess ·	*Sister*
ANDREW ·	Andrew Komierowski ·	*Cousin*
KRYSTYNA ·	Princess Krystyna Lubomirska ·	*Aunt*
STEFAN ·	Prince Stefan Lubomirski ·	*Uncle*
ERIKA ·	Princess Erika Lubomirska ·	*Aunt*
SOPHIE ·	Countess Sophie Rostworowska ·	*Aunt*
ALISIA ·	Sophie's Daughter ·	*Cousin*
ANUSIA ·	Sophie's Daughter ·	*Cousin*
ROSE ·	Countess Rose Potocka ·	*Aunt*
	(Uncle Stefan's sister)	
ROSE ·	Princess Rose Lubomirska ·	*Aunt*
NATALIA ·	Rose's Daughter ·	*Cousin*
ELIZABETH ·	Rose's Daughter ·	*Cousin*
JOSEPH ·	Count Joseph Zoltowski ·	*Uncle*
	(Tatek's brother-in-law)	
HELENA ·	Countess Helena Zoltowska ·	*Cousin*

FAMILY RETAINERS AT ADAMPOL

MAZUR ·	·	*Gardener*
FRANUS ·	Franus Mis ·	*Butler*
WLADEK ·	Wladek Szelongowski ·	*son of the Forester*

Part One

ADAMPOL

Above the entrance to the Zamoyski palace at Adampol, Poland, hangs a coat of arms with a horned goat, a crown, and three lances. Beneath it there is an inscription in gold letters on black marble. It reads,

MAY THESE THREE LANCES
REMIND YOU ALWAYS OF THE
THREE GOALS IN LIFE
FAITH, COUNTRY, HONOR

THE ZAMOYSKI COAT OF ARMS DATES BACK TO 1331, when it was given to an ancestor by the Polish king Wladyslaw Lokietek, who defeated the Teutonic Knights at the battle of Plowce.

This warrior lay dying on the battlefield, pierced by three lances. When the king commiserated with his suffering, the warrior answered: "It hurts less than a bad neighbor."

He survived, and for his bravery King Lokietek knighted him and gave him land and a coat of arms with three lances and the motto *"To Mniey Boli"*—"This Hurts Less."

POLAND—ADAMPOL, 1942

The noise of a car intrudes upon the peace of an early August morning. I glance at my father, Tatek, whose eyes, filling with fear, shift toward the open window. My younger sister, Basia, starts to rise but, seeing Tatek's rigid stare, remains seated.

There is a screech of brakes and the loud slam of doors. Jerome, my brother, a year older than I, is usually cocky and sure of himself; he now looks pale. A spoon clangs onto the table, for Andrew, a younger cousin, had been playing with his breakfast until the doors slammed.

We hear the approaching footsteps. Are there one or two pairs? At first it is hard to tell. They climb the front stairs in unison; then a step misses cadence. There are two of them. What do they want so early in the morning? Like hunting dogs, we have learned over the last three years to listen for the sounds of trouble and be alert to impending uncertainties.

As we wait for the knock, the doors burst open. Tatek, about to rise, sits back, stunned: Gestapo, the most feared.

"From this moment on, this house and the entire estate belong to the Reich. You have two days to get out. Nothing is to be taken. The doors to each room will be sealed by one of us."

As quickly as they entered, they now shout "Heil Hitler," turn, and leave: The Gestapo allow no questions.

I do not hear them go down the stairs, for it is all I can do to hold back my fury. We jump from our chairs and scatter in separate directions, not wanting Tatek, who is still slumped in disbelief, to confirm what we have just heard.

I am sixteen, a young girl with strong emotions. We are being driven from an estate that has belonged to the Zamoyski family for centuries.

I sit on the bench in front of the house, staring into space as if hypnotized. I keep wondering in a numb way how I could say farewell to all those things that were a part of me. The house, all the beautiful woods around with their streams and ponds, the farms with their large fields and meadows, the herds of cattle, and my beloved horses, the thoroughbred mares, back home from their racing career and with their foals. Oh, how I loved it all. And my dogs, and all the servants who were my friends, who had been there for as long as I could remember.

For three years, we have lived at Adampol in the same house with the Germans, who chose it as their army headquarters. While we were allocated only a few rooms of our home, scores of officers and soldiers have trespassed, looting all they could until nothing but bare walls remained. Now our last space is to be taken away.

Leave in two days? To go where? And do what? Not even a chance to ask Mama, as she is away visiting Grandmama. I am scared, and for the first time in my life unsure of myself. I just cannot accept that at this very moment my entire way of life is ending, like a book I have finished and put away on a shelf, never to be read again.

So in two days I will be gone, and away forever from here. I repeat the words over and over to convince myself that it is true. The sun will be shining tomorrow and the next day, and the forest will whisper the same eternal song, but I won't be there—I who am a part of it all. How can I leave it all forever? No, I can't; it just is not possible.

Perhaps the Germans will soon lose the war and I will be able to return to what I love so much, and what is all I know. Maybe all of this is just a nightmare, and maybe I will wake up soon, to find myself in my room, safe and at home to stay.

ADAMPOL, 1929

"Christine, hurry! Jerome, listen to me!"

Mama is pulling my arm so hard that it hurts. I want to go back to sleep in my room, but her insistent voice grows louder. I try to look up at her face but can see only an outline of her head and hair. As a door opens amid the thickening smoke, we hear Jerome. "I'm here, Mama."

"Jerome, take my hand."

"Mama, I want to go back to my room," I say.

"Christine, be still. We must get out quickly."

She tightens her grip on my arm.

"What is that?"

"Something fell."

The smoke in my chest makes me feel sick, and my eyes hurt. Mama is coughing. While Jerome is pulling Mama's arm ahead of us, my feet are almost off the floor. We escape through the hallway, push open the doors, and run toward the steps. There I trip.

"Ouch." My knee hurts. "Please stop."

Mama doesn't seem to hear as we continue down the stairs. I turn to look behind me and see fire coming out of my bedroom window, and Jerome's window, too.

I cling to my mother's skirt, then lean against a big chair. It belongs in the main hall by the fireplace. Now it is on the lawn, getting wet in the rain. The servants run frantically, piling things in the middle of the court-yard. Fire is coming out of all the windows now, even the roof. I edge closer to Jerome while the rain pounds down, bringing with it the sparks that fall around us.

At the far end of the path in the woods stands a statue of the Virgin Mary. While Mama prods us firmly in that direction, I can hear something very big fall behind me, then a scream. The roof is gone.

"Both of you stay here by the Virgin. No matter what happens, don't leave until I come for you."

She sounds so stern. In fright, I lean against the statue. Although we cannot see Mama through the smoke, we can hear her talking to Mazur the gardener, until the fire swells to a roar as the house tumbles in upon itself. The rain makes hissing noises while it turns to steam.

A pane of glass in the greenhouse explodes. Maybe the Virgin will save me, so I try to put my arms around the statue. It does not feel as safe as Mama's skirt.

"Jerome, where's Mama? Will she come back for us?"

"Of course, stupid. She told us to stay here. She'll be back."

When she emerges from the smoke and the rain, her hair, soaked, has fallen down around her shoulders, its folds making little canals for the water. With a tired hand she tries to place it back on top of her head, but it keeps falling.

"Christine, Jerome. I need a beret."

Jerome is wearing a navy blue beret and I am wearing a red one. I take mine off and offer it to her. Why is Jerome taking his off? He can see that I am giving Mama mine.

"Here, Mama, take mine," he says.

"No, Mama, please take mine. I took mine off first."

I try to press my beret into her hand. She takes Jerome's, then quickly disappears into the smoke.

I look at Jerome. I hate him. He is taunting me.

"See, I told you mine was better than yours. She took my beret, not your silly little one."

The main house at Adampol burns to the ground.

1932–1937

Within fifteen months the house was completely rebuilt. Rain had prevented the fire from destroying the flower conservatory, with the three tall palm trees which had originally decorated a room for Czar Alexander. Dziadzio, my grandfather, brought them to Adampol from Mama's family estate at Kruszyna. Subsequently, canaries flew through these trees, free and uncaged.

Mazur, a superb gardener, arranged flowers, bushes, and mosses in mosaics around each of the palms. The mosses, bright red, deep orange, wine, silver, and green, were outlined with gray. The floor of the conservatory became Mazur's tapestry.

A long corridor also spared by the fire, its roof a terrace, occupies the space opposite the conservatory. The main house on one end and the guest house on the other complete the quadrangle.

The estate, one hundred and ten thousand acres, provided much of what was needed to restore the house to its original condition. Wood came from the carefully tended forests which made up much of the acreage. The forty foresters and their families who lived on the estate cut and hammered the beams while the artisans from the village rebuilt the fireplaces. A new heating system was installed, pipes no longer were insulated with leaves and straw, and many rooms were supplied with chimneys to accommodate the necessary tiled woodstoves. For no heating system can keep the larger rooms warm amid the arctic wind of a Polish winter. By the time I was seven the main house seemed old again, as if it had never been destroyed.

It wasn't this way with Rozanka, the castle of Tatek's forefathers, which was burned to the ground in World War I: Only the granite walls remained.

The castle was on a hill overlooking the River Bug. Everything was destroyed by the fire except the painting of the Madonna that hung in the chapel. Tatek did not rebuild Rozanka, because like everyone else after World War I, he had financial difficulties. Rebuilding Adampol was far less costly.

In 1932, this painting of the Madonna was brought from Rozanka to the chapel in Adampol. Many believed it a miracle that it had survived the fire, as even its frame had been burned. A group of servants and my family carried the Madonna from Rozanka to Adampol in a fifteen-mile procession on foot.

I turn away from the house, its memories, to look toward the garden. I remember when I was seven years old, trying to make my voice sound severe, commanding.

There are several children in the strawberry patch. Mazur is yelling at them.

"No, you must not eat the berries or pick them. How many times do I have to chase you away? The countess does not want you here."

The children are from the families of the peasants who live on our estate. Although I do not play with them, I know their faces even when stained with freshly devoured strawberries. Mama has instructed Mazur to keep them out because while picking a few berries they had trampled most of the plants. I watch Mazur carefully, then speak.

"Mazur, they may eat the berries, and if they wish, they may pick more. My mother will not become poor because a few children eat our strawberries."

Mazur turns upon me and I glare back at him. I have no interest in the children or the strawberries, but I want Mazur as well as the children to recognize that I have the same authority to deny or allow as does Mama. For a moment I am not sure what Mazur will do. Patiently he says, "Yes, Miss Countess, they may pick the berries as you say."

Mazur has obeyed my orders. As I walk away, I neither look at the children nor smile. I do wonder: Will Mazur tell Mama? Will I be called to Mama's study for a spanking? The only promises Mama keeps are the spankings.

I decide that even if Mazur does tell Mama and I am punished, it will have been worth it.

The clouds have many different shapes. One looks like a dragon with a huge mouth and a tail with spikes. I shiver. What if it leaps from the sky into my room? I jump back into bed and pull the covers over my head, only to picture the skins of two wolves that Mama shot, as they now hang on the wall with their huge heads and their white teeth. Their eyes, pale and glossy brown, follow me no matter where I stand. Jerome tells me that they can leap off the wall and eat me. They can eat a whole flock of chickens. That *is* true.

As I look out the window again, a half-moon throws light on a cloud formed like a mushroom; such mushrooms are the homes of the dwarfs. When the cloud is almost gone, I wonder if my dwarfs might disappear. I shall write them a letter.

In the morning I am no longer frightened, but very secretive.

"Mama, how do I write 'brass bed'? Please print it for me."

"Dziadzio, will you print the word 'unhappy' for me?"

"Tatek, how do I write 'Please help me'?"
I write:

Dear Dwarfs:

I know you are there under the mushrooms, and I know that you will read my letter. I am very unhappy. I hate my brass bed and I want to ride my horse alone. I don't want to study, I detest adding and counting, and when I read I want to read only about you . . . don't ever tell Mama or Tatek that I wrote to you. Don't tell anyone. I love you very much.

Christine.

When I have an answer to my letter, then I will be happy. The dwarfs will be all mine and I will never introduce them to Jerome or Basia.

Three days pass. I run to the woods every time I can do so without being watched. Always, I find the letter exactly as I left it under the red mushroom. So I worry. Maybe they don't live under that mushroom? Maybe they went away to Warsaw as Tatek so often does?

Shears in hand, Mama walks toward the garden to cut some flowers. Because she talks forever with the gardener about I-don't-know-what I don't usually go with her, but today I decide to join her.

"Mama, do dwarfs live under *all* mushrooms?"

"No, Christine, only under red ones."

"*All* red ones?"

"I guess they don't always live under mushrooms, for if it rains they would get wet."

"But if you wanted to write a letter to the dwarfs, Mama, where would you leave it?"

"Oh, I suppose at the end of the garden under the big stone where we often sit . . . there."

After waiting one entire day, I return to the stone at the end of the garden. My letter is gone. In its place there is another one, written in multicolors on beautiful paper. Even though I cannot read all of their words, I am certain that the dwarfs love me and that they want to write to me.

Clutching my precious letter, I find my grandfather, to help me read it. "Dziadzio, will you please?"

Not waiting for an answer, I climb in his lap and push the letter nervously toward him.

Now, letters come from the dwarfs each time I write. When I ask them questions they always answer, but I still have never seen them.

Mama left for Warsaw this afternoon. I pleaded with her to take me with her so that I could see *Snow White and the Seven Dwarfs*. She said "*No!*"

"I can't walk. My legs won't move," I tell Alisia, my cousin who is also my tutor, when she calls me for dinner.

Grasping my legs, she swings them off the side of the bed and lifts me up. The legs crumble beneath me and I am on the floor. Alisia gasps.

That evening, dinner is sent to my room. When the next afternoon my legs still won't move, Alisia sends for the doctor from town. He enters the room with her, takes my temperature, and asks about my legs. Only when he pricks the bottom of my foot with a pin do I say ouch, but I do not allow my legs to move. I am determined.

As the two of them help me stand I protest, and as soon as they let go I fall on the floor. The doctor carefully examines the muscles in my calves and thighs, then shakes his head and says to Alisia, "I don't know quite yet."

Every day he reappears with a different medicine or new theory. Every night I leap and dance around the room until I hear approaching footsteps. Then I am onto the bed where I "paralyze" my legs. After nine days of paralysis Mama and Tatek decide from Warsaw that I should see a specialist there. My excitement makes it more difficult than ever for me to keep my legs still. I am going to Warsaw! Once there, somehow, I know that I will see *Snow White*.

The specialist at the Warsaw clinic asks, "Tell me, Christine, when did you first notice that something was wrong with your legs? What were you doing? Were you talking with someone?"

"I was talking to Mama. She wouldn't let me go to Warsaw with her to see *Snow White*."

"Why was your mother going to Warsaw?"

"I don't know."

I lie on his examining table, pouring out my desire to see the movie and telling him about my need to affirm the existence of dwarfs.

"Christine, I think I have a cure for you. I am going to put hot packs on your legs. In about an hour they should be better, and then perhaps your mother will take you to the movie."

The doctor talks to Mama in another room.

"Countess Zamoyska, your daughter is fine. She has no trace of atrophy in her legs and must have managed a great deal of exercise in her room while all of you were worried and unaware.

"But Countess, your daughter feels it is very important to see *Snow White and the Seven Dwarfs*. You know, you did help her to believe in these things. Perhaps it would have been better, when you left for Warsaw, if you had told Christine the reason, the death of your brother."

Mama enters the examining room, smiling.

"The doctor tells me that he has found a cure for you."

I swing my legs back and forth as I sit on the edge of the table, hoping that I didn't recover too soon.

"This afternoon, if you can walk, we shall see *Snow White*."

WARSAW, 1938

My persistence accounts for my being in this room with its dark brown rugless floor, curtainless windows, and stark white walls unrelieved by a single picture. Only a crucifix is nailed above the door. Six iron beds with boardlike mattresses are separated by six identical night tables. Metal lockers, each tagged with a name, contain the uniforms which ensure that we appear identical.

Last summer I continually asked Mama troublesome questions about God and sex.

"Christine, this fall we will send you to the Sisters of Nazareth at their school in Warsaw. They will help you find the answers."

Even more adamantly than Mama, the nuns refuse to consider my questions. They have rules that are not only strict, they are senseless. While taking a bath I am required to wear my slip, for it is considered sinful to look at one's own body. Defiantly, I remove my slip when I climb into the tub for my weekly bath. Sister Theresa patrols the bathroom.

"You will do without your bath next week. You have violated the rule about covering your body. Christine, you must learn to obey."

Each morning I along with all the other students kneel on the cold stone floor of the chapel for the required prayers. Sister Theresa, wrinkle-faced and with a curved nose like a parrot's, squawks at me that I must go to confession. To retaliate, I nonchalantly tell the priest that I will not confess to any sins, as I don't feel that I have committed any. I know that he will not give me absolution, and therefore I will not be allowed Communion. Of course, the nuns observe this and are very disturbed. I never answer their many questions.

I feel alone here. Most of the girls, cold and religious like the nuns, are petty, being occupied with small bits of gossip that do not interest me. I am beginning to like one girl, Tekla, who has bright blue eyes and a long black braid that hangs down to the back of her knees. It is her responsibility to look after the school's Saint

Bernard. Sometimes I walk him in Tekla's place. In the afternoon, when the entire school promenades through the park, each of us repeating our rosary, I think about the dog rather than my prayers. We are a long row of geese led by a Saint Bernard!

We are forbidden to talk after bed prayers. At home I was allowed to talk until I fell asleep, and as I see no reason for the silence, I do not observe it. The ever-present Sister Theresa unsuccessfully attempts to quiet me. Thereafter, she disgraces me in front of the other girls by pushing my bed into the hall. As soon as she leaves I jump out of bed and flee, barefoot, up the stairs to the top floor of the building. I decide to hide in one of the classrooms and sneak out after everyone is asleep; tonight I shall run away from school. After locking the door behind me, I wait quietly in the dark. To me, in this room at Nazareth, the sisters do not seem like angels of mercy.

I remember how uncomfortable religion was at Adampol as well. Every Sunday morning the aged village priest said Mass in the family chapel. Then, for two years, a young priest lived with us at Adampol. Priests are supposed to be old and wise and have white hair and large bellies, but this priest, pink-cheeked and blue-eyed, looked like a small boy. Nevertheless, he was our instructor and his responsibility was to prepare Jerome and me for our first confession and Communion.

At my first Communion, in my white veil, new white shoes, and gloves, I finally became equal to Jerome. His first Communion had occurred a year before mine.

When Jerome was nine, he was chosen to be an altar

boy. Considering this to be a great honor, Tatek saw to it that he had been perfectly trained, but Jerome, with his impressive robes, used his new role only to torment me.

"Girls are inferior to boys. They are never allowed to serve at Mass. You are only a girl."

I appealed to the young priest.

He responded, "Believe, Christine, and God will answer all of your prayers."

I prayed and prayed that I could be an altar boy. "Believing" brought no results.

Soon I began to test religious precepts.

For instance, "God must not be mocked."

The family sat like stone images in the front three pews of the Adampol chapel while other people from the estate stood behind them. One morning I quietly made the sign of the cross backward, then upside down. My fear of punishment was so great that I confided in Jerome.

"Oh, Christine, nothing is going to happen. Why do you even bother to do such foolish things?"

In the hallway outside my bedroom at Adampol hung a picture of Christ on the cross. Sometimes Mama formed the sign of the cross when she passed it. One day, I scrutinized this figure with blood flowing from His wounds and taunted, "If You are all-powerful, why do You hang there in misery? Why did You permit Yourself to be so mistreated?"

I glanced around me to make certain that no one was watching; then, staring straight into Christ's eyes, I muttered, "Stupid!" In terror, I raced down the hallway as if chased by a devil. Because I was certain that by morning I might be in hell, I struggled all of that night to remain awake, simply to be sure not to die. The following day, still quite alive, I could not resist repeating once again, "Stupid!"

I am jolted back to this room at Nazareth; the squawks of Parrot Nose and Mother Superior precede the rattling of the door handle.

"Christine, we know that you are in there. Come out, this very instant. God will punish you severely for your transgression."

Reluctantly, I release the lock.

Mama is summoned to Warsaw. All my efforts to escape have been futile. Mother Superior informs me that I will remain until the end of the school year.

The advice, the reprimands proceed as Mama, Tatek, Parrot Nose, and Mother Superior all talk at once. From time to time I nod my head but can only feel my loneliness. Even at Adampol it was lonely. Basia was too young to play with and Jerome, as eldest son and heir to the estate, was away at boarding school. I would only occasionally play with the children from the village, and I went to their school once a year to take an exam so that I might pass on to the next grade.

Tatek's voice contrasts with the squawking of the others.

"Christine, if you will do your schoolwork, listen to Mother Superior, and obey the rules, I will come for you each weekend and bring you to my apartment. What would you think about that?"

His promise catches me by surprise. I wonder if there

are other conditions. One thing is certain. Unlike Mama, Tatek always keeps his promises.

My father's apartment is predominantly blue. Every detail contributes to a harmony of color, so perfect that even the book bindings blend with the tones of blue in the furniture and rugs. The two large armchairs and the ample couch are soft and enfolding; one never wishes to leave their comfort. Occasionally, a small white feather makes its way through the thick, plush cushion cover and rests like a snowflake on one of the dark blue chairs until it is noticed and blown out the window. At night the heavy velvet drapes are drawn to insure our privacy.

At the far end of the living room there is a small bar with sparkling crystal glasses which ring in brilliant tones. Since both Father and his servant, Jozio, smoke, as well as the many guests, the room is often heavy with blue haze. When I am alone, I sometimes lift a cigarette from one of the silver boxes on the side tables. No one suspects me.

Here I not only feel free, but pampered and important. Saturday morning begins when Jozio carries a breakfast tray to my bedroom, where I lie under a thick down cover. We then plan the evening's drinks. Although Father and I always have our dinner in a restaurant or at the racing club, we do invite guests to the apartment for drinks. For such occasions Jozio prepares fancy hors d'oeuvres and a variety of drinks. I arrange the platters and proudly pass them to the guests. I am the hostess and Tatek treats me as such; he stands beside me, tall and thin with black hair and eyes the same blue-gray color as mine. I never mention it to him, but I feel sometimes like his "little wife." He doesn't seem to notice that I am merely thirteen.

Last Saturday night, Tatek gave a dinner party at the Europejski Hotel. Its exquisite restaurant is clothed in velvet and gold; private cubicles provide a living-room atmosphere. When Mama is with us, we are always seated at a special table reserved for her family, the Lubomirskis. However, Tatek and I, along with his friends, sat at a different table. I wore the new dress he gave me, with its low-cut purple elegance, and an amethyst necklace, which I had chosen myself. Tatek allowed me to wear makeup. However, he cautioned me, "Don't tell Mama that you use lipstick, because you *and* I will catch hell for it."

Before the guests were seated I went to the powder room and added to my costume some perfume that I had purchased in the Brothers Jablkowski Department Store. I inadvertently poured most of the bottle on my hair. When I returned to Father and his guests, the fragrance was stunning. Father carefully whispered to me, "Where did you get that perfume? You would smell better if you had rolled with the dogs on a dead fish."

"Please, Tatek, don't say anything in front of all these people."

He laughed and nodded his head as if we had shared an amusing anecdote.

Tatek bought me a small blue bottle of Soir de Paris yesterday, at a perfumery near his apartment.

"Tonight, Christine, one drop. That is enough."

In the clubhouse dining room overlooking the racing track, I feel quite at ease with my one drop of perfume as I meander among the conversations.

"Wanda has the best legs."

The colonel bursts into a loud laugh.

"Legs and beautiful hair."

"A thoroughbred with perfect conformation."

I wonder who owns the horse named Wanda, for she is surely not one of ours.

"Expensive mare, but the smoothest on the entire track."

"Whose mare is she?" I ask, and all the men burst into laughter.

"Does she belong to one of you gentlemen?"

The colonel, his hand on mine, with a serious face but a choking voice, attempts to answer.

"Young lady, we all own Wanda, as she is mutual property and we each share part of her winnings. She is a fine mare, slow to start, but accelerates toward the finish, and is willing to run under any handicap."

"You mean she runs under heavy weight?"

The colonel looks at the large-bellied man opposite him, shakes his head from side to side, and answers, "Heavy indeed, very heavy."

Now they all roar with laughter, and I feel that it is at my expense. Eventually, it occurs to me that Wanda has two legs.

In the apartment's entry hall there is a guest book. Each visitor signs it with a few words. One of Tatek's friends wrote, "You are a wonderful host and father to

Christine. Keep her from becoming a nun." Beneath it
I signed, "Don't worry, I WON'T."

At Adampol, I had been afraid of Tatek, for as he was
seldom present, he seemed remote and stern. His yes
and his no sounded so final, so absolute. In Warsaw I
have come to trust him as my companion.

When I left the convent school in mid-June of 1939 to
return to Adampol for vacation, I anticipated a wonderful
stretch of summer with my horses and my dogs. I soon
discovered that my satisfaction with nature and animals
had diminished. I want, now, to be introduced to young
men, to hear Warsaw compliments and plan parties with
dresses, jewels, and perfume.

Tatek has helped me to enter a new world. I can't
wait for tomorrow.

We are to have a houseful of visitors this summer. Every
other year we go to Kruszyna, my mother's family estate,
to spend our summer holidays with Mama's parents, her
in-laws, and all the cousins. This year they are all coming
to Adampol. It is almost like an exchange program; one
year in Adampol, one in Kruszyna. I consider Kruszyna
my second home. It is a very old castle, dating back to
the 1300s. I have often felt it was haunted, with all the
creaks and noises the old building makes.

Off the main hall there is a white marble staircase
lined with portraits of Polish kings glaring sternly at

you as you climb the stairs. They always give me the creeps, and I race up and down the steps as quickly as I can.

Kruszyna is one of the many so-called Rosary castles, which were built as fortresses every twenty kilometers, with secret connecting underground corridors, around the town of Czestochowa and the church of the Black Madonna, so sacred to all Poles. It was a church of miracles, Poles believed. The Madonna had thrown her mantle across a moat and saved the convent and the church from Poland's enemies long ago.

At Kruszyna no one was ever denied food or lodging, from kings and presidents to the poor and homeless. There was always a place for everybody; it was always a full house. My grandmother's brother was Maurice Zamoyski. After World War I, with Ignacy Paderewski and other patriots, he helped to form the new free Poland. For over a hundred years Poland had been partitioned between Russia, Germany, and Austria. Between the two world wars was the only time in memory we were a free country. Later he became Poland's ambassador to France. Once he told my mother that the true aristocrat is one who treats kings and peasants with the same respect. This applied to both Kruszyna and Adampol. It was not uncommon for a cousin or an uncle to come to Kruszyna for lunch and remain for several years.

My grandfather, along with his brothers, was a great patron of the arts. They always helped many artists develop their talents and gave them financial support.

There were singers and violinists, pianists and painters who stayed in Kruszyna for many months and benefited from the generosity of Dziadzio, my grandfather.

Artur Rubinstein, the great pianist, writes in his autobiography, *My Young Years:*

But, glory be to God, as the Irish say, a new *deus ex machina* in the person of the Prince Ladislas Lubomirski appeared out of nowhere at just the right moment. I noticed in the newspaper that he was about to arrive in Warsaw for a conference with his brother Stanislav, the banker, and my unfailing instinct told me that it was of utmost importance for me to see him. I entered the restaurant of the Hotel d'Europe at lunchtime with the air of one who is expected by friends, when a loud voice called: "Panie Arturze!" [which means "Mr. Arthur"] "What are you doing in Warsaw?" It was the Prince sitting at the table with his brother and another man. I greeted him, pretending great surprise. "I am waiting for the opening of the Philharmonic concerts," I said. "But you should be heard in great cities, in Berlin, Vienna, Rome, Paris. To stay in Warsaw is not good enough for your great talent."

"I would love to be able to follow your advice, Prince, but it is impossible for me," I said, and gave him an idea of what it would cost to give concerts in these cities when one is not well known. "Unless you want to become my manager, Prince?" I added playfully. "And why not?" he answered quite seriously.

"I shall deposit ten thousand rubles ($5,000) in my brother's bank. You can draw on this sum to cover the expenses of these concerts," and without losing time, he put this agreement on paper, signed it and handed it to the third man at the table, a Mr. Gintout, the director of the Lubomirskis' bank. "Here is to your success," they toasted me with the last sip of wine, and without listening to my thanks, they got up and left. I was in heaven. This was the great moment of my life! Nothing more to worry about!

When once my grandfather was complimented on his generosity to artists, he replied, "Without my money, the great talent of Artur Rubinstein would have survived anyway; but my money, without the talent of Rubinstein, could never have brought such pleasure to the world."

SEPTEMBER 1939, ADAMPOL

September 1, 1939. Poland and the Third Reich are at war. Adampol resembles a railroad station filled with travelers who must stay for a night or two, only to move on to another uncertain destination. A seemingly endless stream of refugees continues to arrive in horse-drawn wagons, on foot, a few in cars. We greet a cousin who appears in a truck containing wooden cases filled with porcelains and paintings which are then piled in a hallway. Concurrently, a friend is burying his silver and jewels in the forest. Most of the exiles clutch only meager possessions and perhaps a small amount of food; yet inevitably these people are accompanied by the family pet. Dogs of every breed and station roam randomly, as lost and confused as their masters.

I detest the chaos in our house. I find strangers sleeping on our couches, in our chairs, in virtually any corner of every room. The less fortunate rest uneasily on the ground outside. They litter the gardens with scraps of paper, while their dusty cartons and suitcases cover the floors which were once kept spotless and shining.

We have managed to feed these people, often as many as three hundred a day, by slaughtering our pigs, chickens, turkeys, and cows. It is senseless, after all, to preserve the animals for the Germans. Our servants prepare huge caldrons of meat-based soups containing vegetables, potatoes, and noodles.

I observe the disarray of crystal and china and then gaze at the human victims with their blood-soaked bandages. They embody a reality I had not yet seen. With compassion for their tragedy, I move among them, drawn by their stories, transfixed by the intimate descriptions of the horrors they have endured.

Occasionally one of my cousins figures among the masses who seek Adampol for a temporary haven. The cousins remain; so finally there are ten of us who roam about together doing quite as we please. We celebrate the "wonderful war" that has caused schools to be closed, protecting us from returning to our respective Nazareths. At times we gather on the terrace with brooms and sticks for a mock battle against the Germans.

■ ■ ■

Basia's face beams as she hurries toward Mama.

"Andrew is at the railroad station and Tatek has taken the Chrysler to bring him home."

Cousin Andrew's mother died when he was only three. He then lived with us for long stretches of time, so naturally became a "brother" and a "son" within our own family. Andrew was a good-natured child, close to Basia in age and temperament, and he was always pampered. I was jealous of all the attention he got. He had an exasperating habit of always being totally precise. You would ask him a yes or no question and he would give you a two-hour answer. But we all loved him. The fact that his home, Komierowo, now in German hands, was the locus of the most fierce of battles aroused grave concern in Mama and Tatek and cast a shadow over all.

As we sit down for lunch, our relief that Andrew is with us, alive and whole, is yoked with the anxious realization that his father is not. Tatek asks, "Andrew, tell us now, where is your father? What happened?"

Although exhausted, Andrew manages to narrate a long, exasperating, detailed account.

"I was on vacation when, on August twenty-ninth, my father telephoned me and told me to return immediately to Komierowo, my home. Father wanted to see me before sending me to Adampol, away from the German-Polish front. I returned the same day with my tutor, Izabela, and on August thirtieth my father, Izabela, and I left by car for Torun. We stayed in a hotel that night. I remember most that it was very expensive and that we had chicken and fries, my favorite meal. Now let me see, how much did it cost? I think—"

Finally Father interrupts. "Oh, for God's sake, Andrew, get to the point."

Then Mama. "Andrew, all right, all right, but what happened to your father?"

"I will get to it. Wait, I must tell you everything. . . ."

And he does!

No one interrupts Andrew this time, as we realize that it is futile. Tatek merely grumbles under his breath.

". . . We went to the railroad station and boarded the train for Warsaw. I begged my father to come with us. I was afraid to be separated from him but he seemed unaware.

" 'Komierowski belongs in Komierowo. If the Germans do come to our home I will show them the Iron Cross that I received in 1917. They will bow to me for that.'

"The train, pulling additional cars filled with army recruits, twice was strafed and bombed by German aircraft. Izabela and I lay flat on the floor while bullets pierced the windows above our heads. One of the cars at the end of the train was blown off the tracks. I heard the screams but dared not lift my head. . . ."

Andrew shudders as he finishes his story.

Mama reassures him. "You are safe now, Andrew, but do you know where your father is? What were his plans?"

"I don't know, but I am sure the Germans could not harm him. They will respect my father!"

I believe Andrew. The next day we celebrate with another party, for Andrew has joined the "no-school" contingent of cousins at Adampol.

■ ■ ■

═GERMAN ARMY ATTACKS POLAND;═ CITIES BOMBED, PORT BLOCKADED; DANZIG IS ACCEPTED INTO REICH

BERLIN, FRIDAY, SEPT. 1—Charging that Germany had been attacked, Chancellor Hitler at 5:11 o'clock this morning issued a proclamation to the army declaring that from now on force will be met with force and calling the armed forces "to fulfill their duty to the end." The text of the proclamation reads:

To the defense forces:

The Polish nation refused my efforts for a peaceful regulation of neighborly relations; instead it has appealed to weapons.

Germans in Poland are persecuted with a bloody terror and are driven from their homes. The series of border violations, which are unbearable to a great power, prove that the Poles no longer are willing to respect the German frontier. In order to put an end to this frantic activity no other means is left to me now than to meet force with force.

"Battle for Honor"

German defense forces will carry on the battle for the honor of the living rights of the re-awakened German people with firm determination.

I expect every German soldier, in view of the great tradition of eternal German soldiery, to do his duty until the end.

Remember always in all situations you are the representatives of National Socialist Greater Germany!

Long live our people and our Reich!
Berlin, Sept. 1, 1939
ADOLF HITLER.

The New York Times, *September 1, 1939*

THE FIRST FLIGHT, 1939

"He is frightfully thin. I tried to feed him this morning, but after eating two bites he fled, almost crazed, to circle again each wagon in search of his master. I don't think I could ever leave my dog like that, no matter how quickly I had to run to save my life," I exclaim.

To calm me down, Mama tells me the story of how she saved a whole litter of borzois. It happened in 1905 when she was ten years old. Czar Alexander had an estate near Kruszyna. One day his hunting borzois got loose and killed a small boy in the village. They had been chasing his pet rabbit; the boy grabbed the rabbit and hid it in his jacket, the dogs tore them both to bits.

Furious about the tragedy, the Czar ordered all his borzois shot. Their kennel keeper was the brother of the forester employed at Kruszyna. Through his brother, the kennel keeper sent a message to Mama saying that many puppies were going to be killed unless she would secretly adopt them. Of course it was breaking the order of the Czar, but Mama did so without any hesitation, took all the puppies, and saved their lives.

We pick the few remaining garden vegetables. Just as I look up at Mama's face to respond, we are startled by Tatek frantically waving his arms as he rushes toward us.

"What's wrong, Tatek? What now?"

"One of our generals and his staff officers are here. The Army is preparing a line of defense at the River Bug, seven miles away. We must leave Adampol."

"No, Tatek!"

Mama crosses herself as we hurry toward the house. Although the general and his officers greet us with great kindness, their underlying tone remains ominous.

"Countess Zamoyska, I am afraid that you will have to leave Adampol, tomorrow night at the very latest. I must insist that *everyone* vacate. We are certain that the Germans have chosen this area as a major target."

While I shudder and Tatek looks aghast, Mama replies with a graciousness that conceals her distress.

"Thank you. We all thank you for warning us."

Mama and Tatek convey the urgency of the general's orders to the refugees, tired of flight. Dismayed by the interruption of their brief moment of safety, the caravan of homeless wanderers nonetheless moves on. Either in haste or perhaps because of a deepening inner fatigue, they often abandon many of their belongings, now scattered about.

Tatek summons his large family to the dining room, where we plan a strategy for moving. There are almost fifty of us, including cousins and servants. We have four cars, a capacity for twenty. The older people and the children will leave in the cars shortly after sundown. The rest, led by my parents, are to begin with the wagons early in the morning.

Our destination is an estate near the Russian border, approximately three hundred miles from Adampol. Tatek's cousin, Isabella Radziwill, has offered her home, Mankiewicze, which is far enough east to be a safe place for all of us. We accept her invitation. It seems the only thing to do.

So in preparation we eat an early supper. The dining room, now devoid of transient refugees, seems strangely empty. For a brief instant, all is peaceful as evening falls on Adampol. The brilliant red sun sets.

"What is that?" I ask Tatek, staring at a blazing sky.

"The sawmills are burning, Christine."

Flames reach higher, then the huge pitch tanks explode. Yes, the Germans have bombed the mill.

"Christine, you must come to the car now."

"Mama," I plead, "let me go with you. Please, I want to go with you and Tatek in the wagons, not in the cars."

"The cars are safer," she answers, while gently stroking the back of my hair.

I cannot accept the reality that we must run from an enemy we have not seen. I want to hide in our forests.

Mama does not consider my suggestions for she is totally occupied with the loading of the cars.

Babcia, Dziadzio, Jerome, Basia, myself, and the driver are crammed into the family Buick. Tucked beneath our feet is a small suitcase and a parcel of food. There is room for nothing else. Bunia, Andrew, my father's sister, my uncle Joseph Zoltowski, and his daughter, my cousin Helena, fill the second car. Uncle Stefan, Aunt Krystyna, and their sons, Stas and Jas, along with Cousin Isabella Radziwill and five other cousins, assign themselves to the two remaining vehicles.

I refuse to look back or wave as the cars set off down the road, one following the other. We pass endless lines of wagons, hundreds of people plodding on foot. Finally, through the entire night, I peer out at shadows. Occasionally, when the car comes to a stop, a face pushes flat against the window. Then I feel dazed, nauseated, afraid; I have never liked the darkness.

Even in such a plight, the morning sun does appear, and we become hungry for breakfast. I take a sandwich from the food basket, then pass it to my grandmother. Now I am able to see more than shadows. We pass a tiny village, a row of thatch-roofed huts, a solitary store, and a church with its parishioners assembled in the foreground. I had forgotten that it was Sunday.

The many cars in front of us decrease their speed until finally all are stopped. We hear a voice repeat, "At least a half-hour wait. Big truck turned over in the road. No way around it."

And then from the sky, a crescendo of roaring motors.

"Quick, out of the car!" Uncle Stefan shouts. "Go into the fields. Scatter behind the cottages; run, run!"

My grandparents, stiff and sore from the long, tedious ride, hold the rails of a broken fence for support. Aunt Krystyna dashes to Dziadzio, and taking him under her arm, helps him to walk. Stumbling behind, Babcia follows as quickly as she can. Natalia and Elizabeth already are in the field.

"Down, everybody, down; cover your faces," Uncle Stefan commands in a voice filled with fear and panic. We fall to the ground.

I turn my head just enough to see the German planes descend; they almost touch the church steeple. I cover my head. Now only sounds. *Tatatatatatatata*, machine guns. They stop for a moment, circle, and then *tatata-tatata*. After the second pass the sounds diminish; the planes, decreasing in size, fly toward the horizon.

Silence, then a broken sob. I look. Red stains on her white dress, a little girl is lying very still. She was too small to run. I have never seen a dead child before.

We no longer drive by day, but hide the cars beneath a grove of trees, well camouflaged with leaves, then start out after dark. The roads are clogged, making the driving intolerably slow. At times a fierce blaze of red or perhaps a glow less shocking pierces our dark monotony. Another village, burning.

Finally, on the fifth night, we reach Mankiewicze. The palace, filled beyond capacity with refugees, boxes, and homeless dogs, looks much as Adampol did. Fortunately for us, the manager of one of the palace's multitude of farms has recently been dismissed, so we are able to live in his vacated house. Jerome, Andrew, Basia, and I, along with Uncle Stefan, Aunt Krystyna, and their sons, and Aunt Rose Lubomirska and her daughters Natalia and Elizabeth, all settle in this crude manager's house on the farm called Dolin.

There is no indoor toilet and the only source of water is a hand pump outside the kitchen door, but there are four bedrooms, which certainly offer more comfort than would a bed on the palace grounds. In this simple house we cook our own breakfast but walk to the palace for our other meals. While most of the refugees eat wherever they can find an unoccupied spot, we join the family at the long carved-oak table in the dining room. The embroidered linen tablecloth, priceless china, crystal glasses, and sterling serving dishes fail to camouflage the paucity of food.

The days repeat one another. A week goes by while, like those abandoned dogs at Adampol, I keep my post at the crossroads and search every wagon. My parents should have reached Mankiewicze. I continually recollect the small girl dead near the church and I wonder. . . .

Uncle Stefan is setting the wood fire to cook our breakfast of bread and bitter cocoa when our driver, Poroszewski, bursts in.

"All but the elderly prince and princess are gone!"

"What? Gone where?" Jerome asks nervously.

"Everyone is gone but your grandparents."

"Why?" asks Uncle Stefan.

Poroszewski is breathless.

"I did not know that they had left. I stayed, as you know, in the servants' quarters and only learned of their departure this morning when I went to the palace. Prince Lubomirski told me that although he himself did not hear it, the Russian invasion of Poland was announced on the radio early last evening. He was not told until Princess Radziwill had prepared to leave early this morning. She informed Princess Lubomirska that she would escape back to the west, and that the princess was welcome to make use of whatever was in the palace. The Russians are now within a few miles of us."

Uncle Stefan's face reddens with anger.

"Poroszewski, are you sure that they are all gone? Aunt Mary, Bunia?" I demand.

"Yes, Miss Countess, everyone except your grandparents."

Uncle Stefan interrupts: "Our cars, quickly. We still may have time to outdistance the Russians. Poroszewski, you and I will go to the palace for Dziadzio and Babcia and bring back both cars. Hurry!"

"No . . . we cannot!" Poroszewski looks beaten and dejected. "The gas from the cars has been drained. There is no gas."

"Who did that?"

"I don't know. There were many people at the palace. Someone . . ." His voice trails off.

"Why the hell didn't one of them tell us that the Russians invaded? They all knew it since last night!"

Finding his voice, Poroszewski speaks with uncharacteristic anger. "It doesn't seem right. Princess Radziwill knew it before you had dinner with her. The radio announcement was made early in the evening."

My parents have not appeared. Now the Russians. With Germans rolling over us from the west and Russians stomping on us from the east, we will never be free again. I have no doubt, now, that Poland is lost. I hate everyone, especially the selfish cowards in my own family who ran early this morning and left us here, stranded.

"Sons of bitches, cowards, pigs," I scream in an uncontrolled rage. Uncle Stefan mutters other invectives.

"I am going back to Adampol on foot," says Poroszewski, "to be with my wife and children."

"I'm going with you. Take me, Poroszewski."

"No, Christine," Uncle Stefan and Poroszewski shout in unison.

"No, Miss Countess, I cannot take you. The way is long and uncertain."

Uncle Stefan turns to me. "Christine, don't go. I need your help."

But I need to find Mama and Tatek, to know if they are alive. Aunt Krystyna is ill and Dziadzio and Babcia are so old. . . .

"Yes, I will stay."

Uncle Stefan decides that it is best for us to walk to Stolin, the nearest town and railroad station, where we will attempt to find space on a train to Lwow, a large city in the southeast of Poland. Because such a journey is too arduous for Dziadzio and Babcia, we take them only as far as Stolin. Here Uncle Stefan finds a room in a small lodging house, where it is most unlikely that anyone will discover their identity. Now that the Russians have freed every unsavory character held in the prisons, the first targets of the discharged criminals' rampage are likely to be the large landowners, particularly aristocrats such as the Lubomirskis.

Will I ever see them again . . . ?

"What we did to them landlords. You should have been there. We dragged them out of the house, made them crawl, we did, them Zamoyskis." My ears, dulled by the rhythmic click of the train, are instantly alerted. "With pitchforks in 'em they bleed just like anyone else. They look the same dead as any corpse, them with their fancy ways."

The ex-convict, drunk with vodka and bravado, tells his tale. Basia sleeps; Jerome and Andrew become rigid as white marble statues. Terrible fear is about to cause me to scream. Uncle Stefan turns upon me a gaze so riveting that it fuses an iron rod in my back. While never relenting his rigid command, he simultaneously smiles at the raging criminal. He expects me to smile too. I smile.

"Got them good, did you?" says Uncle Stefan.

"Yep, killed them all! Made that pompous bastard watch while we did in his wife and the rest of them, then we done it to him, too."

Mama and Tatek dead! The stranger, wallowing in his liquor and thirst for blood, makes it sound so certain. Please, no! Yet it might be so.

For two days and two nights we must stay on this glutted train, unable to escape the presence of such abomination. Without food or water, we stand the interminable hours, sandwiched body to body, legs swollen, inhaling the sweat, the cheap vodka, the breath of hatred from the many who are drunk. Repeatedly, I am forced to conceal my loathing, to assume a fictitious pose; yet, the moment that I first smiled at the man who claimed to have murdered my parents, I knew that I could carry off any deception that might be required of me.

The railroad station in Lwow overwhelms us. Festive red banners hang on every wall, partnered by portraits of Stalin. Loudspeakers blare out Russian songs. Perhaps this is what Moscow is like?

We abruptly leave this perplexing scene to seek help from Uncle Stefan's brother. His wife, Erika, with her swollen, tear-filled eyes, tells us that her husband had been captured the first day of the Russian invasion; she does not even know where he is detained. Despite her anxiety and fear, she devotes herself to exploring possible living quarters in various parts of the city. Mr. and Mrs. Bielski, old friends of the family, take in the four of us, along with Uncle Stefan and his family. They give us three small rooms in their villa, which houses several other refugees as well as two Russian officers. We have little comfort and no privacy.

Each gray day, more hopeless than the last, brings an increase in arrests of innocent people. I continually worry about my parents. The scenes of horror told by the murderer on the train haunt my nights with dreams of death and blood.

My only defense is physical work. I both nurse Aunt Krystyna, who now has viral pneumonia, and assume a position as the family cook. My cooking, though it leaves much to be desired, is better than nothing at all. My specialty is meatloaf, often made with no meat or with meat that tastes very peculiar. None would be surprised if it was dog or cat, but we agree not to discuss the ingredients.

After dinner, Uncle Stefan regularly listens to the BBC from a radio hidden under the bed in the Bielskis' room. When he quietly asks Jerome, Basia, and me to come to his room, I know that something dreadful has happened. First I think of Mama and Tatek, Dziadzio and Babcia . . . but why isn't Andrew here with us, too? Uncle Stefan closes the door.

"What I am about to tell you, you must not reveal to Andrew. It might be a mistake but—" Uncle Stefan's voice cracks. He continues, "I have just heard on the BBC that the chamberlain to the Pope, Tom Komierowski, was executed by the Germans."

"Andrew's father dead too. Jesus and Mary," whispers Jerome.

For one whole day we keep the secret, sniffling in the dark corners of the house so that Andrew will not see us. Finally, Basia can hold her tongue no longer. She asks Andrew to join her in the toilet, the only private place in the entire house. There she tells him about the news broadcast.

Months later we learned the whole story. Andrew's father returned to Komierowo, but then fled to the woods, where he was hauled in by members of the German

Army. They found he had a pistol tucked in his jacket. They hit him with the butt of a rifle, knocking him to the ground, then shot him in the head.

"No, no, *no!*" shrieked Andrew. "I do not believe you. It is not true!"

Wladek, the son of our forester, volunteered to cross the German and Russian lines in an attempt to find us. He questioned many people, and by uncannily placing together fragments of truth, he actually found us. Wladek was a bit unusual.

"My precious one, I bring you greetings from Adolf Hitler," he says to me.

He gestures extravagantly as he makes a deep bow, his hair brushing the floor.

Amazed, incredulous, I ask the specter, "How is it that you are here? When did they die? Wladek, are you actually here?"

"Die? Who died?"

"Oh, Wladek, please, you know, you must know about Mama and Tatek."

"Little Countess, they are quite alive, sustained by our beloved Adampol."

"Could this be the truth?"

"Indeed, I had considerable conversation with them less than two months ago."

"Are they alive, alive, *alive?*"

"*They* are alive."

For two months we have lived with the weight, the

loneliness, the grief of their deaths . . . and now they are alive!

Wladek continues in his peculiar, flowery speech.

"They have received no communication, heard not the slightest account, had no idea of your dwelling place since we left Adampol around the tenth of September."

"They must be so worried."

"Not for long. I will return to our Adampol within three days and I will bring your parents greetings from Joseph Stalin!"

Mama had given him a letter, a proof of his truth; in its brevity, it merely expressed the hope that we were well and that we would write to her.

Uncle Stefan, Andrew, Basia, Jerome, and I all continue to inundate the exhausted Wladek with our questions.

"But what happened to Mama and Tatek? You were with them in the wagons. Why didn't they come to Mankiewicze?"

"Be patient, be patient, I will reenact for you the entire story."

Wladek, with his thick hair that appears never to have seen a comb or brush, and his pale eyes that often stare into distant places, begins his account.

"The cars left Adampol. Those remaining, having no transportation or certain destination, joined your mother and father in a caravan of seven wagons. Among them were Alisia and her family, Mr. Wladyslaw Walter, who is of course the well-known actor from Warsaw . . . a town official from the north with his large family, and a woman about to have her baby . . . I can't remember them all.

"It took twenty-four hours to ready the wagons, to make provisions, to find the salt. Every wagon carried salt, the currency the peasants valued most, in order to secure them as guides through the marshes.

"Each wagon was pulled by two horses. Your mother's wagon had, in addition, two racehorses attached at the side—you know, the racing mares that were your mother's favorites. It was a burdensome procession. Because the bridge was blown out at the River Bug, we had to take the horses through the water in pitch darkness. Only the countess was skillful, for none of the others had actually handled horses.

"We reached a village, offered salt to pay the necessary guide. At night he walked in front of the leading wagon with a small lamp; it swayed back and forth with each of his steps. The countess drove, watching that light hour upon hour, until eventually no matter where she looked she could see nothing but a swaying light.

"When the sun rose we were traveling close to the edge of the open marshes and so we decided to take cover in a nearby forest. Midway toward our destination, with no cover of trees or darkness, we heard the roar of planes overhead: a squadron of German aircraft flying like a flock of geese. Two of the planes banked to the right and flew right over the caravan, spraying their *tatatatatatat* of machine-gun fire. Then, having completed their 'military mission' against women, old people, and expectant mothers, they straightened their wings and 'heroically' flew back to their squadron."

Wladek, animated and indignant, stands very straight when he is angry at the Germans.

"Was anyone hit?" I interrupt.

"No, we were all alarmed, but quite all right."

Wladek continues without missing a breath. "For two nights we followed the same pattern. We traveled through darkness and withdrew into the forests during the light hours. The third day the German planes flew directly over our camouflage. They did not see the wagons, but we watched them bomb the village. The horses went wild in pandemonium. They reared and kicked at the wagons. It took hours to calm them down.

"All were exhausted before we began our third evening's journey on a road which became increasingly treacherous and narrow. The wagons silently followed one another until we heard a horror-filled shriek from the very end of the line. All wagons halted simultaneously while the startled occupants rushed to the source of the noise. Mr. Walter's wagon was turned over on its side, while the horse struggled, to no avail, to right it. Mr. Walter, a small, crumpled figure in the ditch, howled without restraint.

" 'Mr. Walter, what happened, have you been shot?'

" 'Are you injured? In what way?'

" 'Have you broken bones? Are you able to speak?'

" 'I am lying in nettles!' "

We all laugh as Wladek continues.

"We laughed too. But that same night the countess's wagon slipped from a small bridge. Your mother tried to keep it upright, but it was too heavy and fell to the side, crushing her ankle. Her foot swelled within her high boot. Until the boot was finally cut off days later, she was in agony."

All shudder at the thought of Mama's broken foot. Wladek continues.

"We left the marshes to follow a major route almost halfway between Adampol and Mankiewicze, not knowing that the Russians were invading Poland from the east. The sky was silent.

"In early evening we reached the town of Kamien Koszyrski, then stopped in the churchyard. While your father, Walter, and Alisia's brother, Stas, went to the center of town to buy food, your mother, maneuvering on one leg, somehow managed to feed and water the horses. Hearing a heavy pounding on the earth, she instinctively turned. Your father, racing toward the wagons, shouted, 'Harness the horses immediately. We are returning to Adampol.'

" 'The horses cannot survive without resting.'

" 'The hell with the horses, we are leaving. The Red Army has invaded Poland and is advancing rapidly.'

" 'But what about the children? My parents?' asked the countess.

" 'Don't worry about them. I met a fellow in town who was also at Mankiewicze. He says he saw everyone leaving, heading toward the German-occupied territories. They must have passed us on that damn road. With all the refugees, we didn't see them, nor they us.'

"Once again the wagons trailed one another through the darkness. When we reached Adampol, we were startled by its occupants. . . . Your father's sister, each of her family, all crowded the terrace, but there was no sight of you children. Your mother, half smiling, but with an uneasy feeling, asked, 'Where are the children?'

"Silence.

" 'Where are Stefan, Krystyna, my parents?'

"Silence. . . . Then a voice from the crowd, like a hammer blow.

" 'We had to leave them behind.'

"The countess, stooped and limping, walked past them all and went to her room. Your father followed, but as he passed his family he looked at them with disgust and anger.

" 'Cowards!' "

A long, motionless quiet prevails as Wladek finishes his story. Finally, he breaks the silence.

"If it would not be rude of me, I am very hungry."

While I rush to bring Wladek some soup, I have already determined to go with him, to go home.

Aunt Krystyna says no. She is afraid to let me cross, illegally, the Russian-German border, to go north to Adampol. After much pleading on my part, she consents with one stipulation.

"I will write to your mother, and if she replies that she wishes you to come home, I will permit you to."

I am not sure that I can wait that long.

Wladek assures, "I will carry the letter to the countess and will be back to convey you safely to Adampol."

He leaves, with a promise to return in less than ten days, surely before Christmas.

On December twenty-second Wladek delivers Mama's

letter. She would like us to come, she says, but asks that Uncle Stefan and Aunt Krystyna make the decision. Is it safe?

"You cannot go. It's too dangerous. What if you were caught?" says Aunt Krystyna.

"Why should we be caught?"

"So many have been caught . . . and disappeared."

"That does not mean that we would be."

Jerome intervenes. "We should stay here. At least we are still alive and together. To walk across the border in all that snow . . ."

"Well, Andrew," I say, "do you want to go or don't you?"

"I will do what the rest will do. I won't take sides."

Basia looks in the other direction, refusing to say a word.

"Well, I am going. I was your cook and your nurse, Aunt Krystyna. If I hadn't helped, you would be dead. Then I could go home."

"Oh, for God's sake, shut up, Christine." Jerome retorts. "How can you say such things?"

I feel ashamed; I love Aunt Krystyna and don't wish her dead.

"I won't hold you," Aunt Krystyna says. "If you feel so strongly, you had better return to Adampol."

"Well," says Jerome, "if she's going, we'll all go. I hope we make it."

We board the afternoon train heading toward the Russian-German border. This was the infamous Ribbentrop-Molotov line, by which Hitler and Stalin partitioned Poland between themselves in 1939. As the train pulls forward we look out at Uncle Stefan and Aunt Krystyna, their somber faces. We too are pensive, leaving them behind, abandoning the safety of being with them. Wladek seems quite confident that all will be fine. I believe him because I need to.

We see no evidence of Russian soldiers when we leave the train one mile before reaching the border. The night is crystal; its full moon allows one to see great distances. Russian patrols should be easily visible, but so might we. Basia's frozen feet and tired legs soon balk and become immobile.

Just before reaching the border Basia says, "Set me down, Jerome, I can walk now. I feel better." Jerome sets down his frozen burden, exhausted.

The border is just ahead. We start to run. Unseen but impenetrable, a Russian patrol commands us to halt.

Andrew mutters, "Shit."

Jerome echoes, "Shit."

"We are escaping the Germans. We want to live under the Russians," Wladek barks in fluent Russian.

"You cannot cross the border like this," says a Russian.

"You have I.D. cards?" asks another.

"No, we have nothing," Wladek replies.

"Sit down. There in the snow," they order us.

We do as we are told. Basia reaches for an apple in her little bag. A Russian soldier, suspecting a gun, jumps at her, pointing a bayonet at her stomach. Basia looks at him with a childish sneer, takes the apple, and sticks it on the bayonet. The other Russians burst into coarse laughter. Only Wladek realizes the danger she is in. The Russian soldier, grasping his bayonet, hesitates. Will he ... Then a shout, and another group, caught like ourselves, is herded with us. We are told to march forward, toward the neutral zone, a belt about five hundred feet wide dividing German territory from Russian.

Jerome, Andrew, and Wladek are pushed inside a small shack. The rest of us are ordered, "Go back where you came from."

Another shout: "Go back to the German zone."

The Russians detain the men but send the women back. We walk across the neutral zone and in a few steps are back on German-occupied territory. The lights of a small village beckon ahead.

"Come, Basia, let's go there, to one of the houses with a fire. You are cold, Basia?"

"Yes, but I can manage on my own."

Her voice quavers, and I realize that Basia is now my responsibility. I must bring her home to our parents and I must do it by myself. Jerome is not here to help.

In a peasant's hut I leave Basia safe near the warm stove. Then, resisting the heat of the stove, which makes me tired and sleepy, I pace back and forth between the cottage and the interrogation shack. Through the windows I can see Jerome and Andrew against the wall. I do not dare to cross over to the Russian zone. I have heard so many stories about the Russians, their tortures and defilements, their rapings and total lack of morality.

The wind grows colder as I pace back and forth, wishing for their escape. It is midnight. Basia is safe; Andrew, Jerome, and Wladek are in the Russian sector. I walk slowly, then fall down in the snow, but am too tired to get up. Perhaps I'll sleep, just for a moment.

First dim voices, then two German soldiers force me to stand.

"Walk, *Fräulein*, walk. You must walk to the barn."

"No, I don't want to go to the barn. Please take me to that cottage with my sister."

"No, Fräulein."

They know the pain of frostbite and refuse to take me where it will be too warm too soon. There is a tingling, followed by violent, knifelike throbbing as the circulation returns. I scream with pain. The Germans carefully pack ice and snow on the white spots on my legs. They seem caring toward me. A doctor arrives, examines me, gives me a shot of morphine and "some pills for later." I feel sleepy again. Some long while later, free of pain, I walk to the cottage where my young sister sleeps. At fourteen, I have had my first direct contact with the German Army, the enemy.

I wake still groggy from morphine and pills. By impulse I leave the cottage and cross the clearing to try to see Andrew, Jerome, and Wladek; they are no longer in the interrogation shack. I think they have been moved—no, escaped, perhaps, and have already started for Warsaw. I cannot worry about it any longer.

Basia and I take a train to Warsaw, then another to Adampol. We are repeatedly sidetracked because of

German military trains and delayed by work crews repairing the tracks damaged by bombings. My impatience is a torment. It is the day before Christmas. Will we ever be home again?

At Wlodawa, our village station, I ask one of the owners of the horse-drawn sleighs if he will take us to Adampol, assuring him that my family will pay him well for his trouble. He bundles the two of us beneath warm furs and we begin our final seven-kilometer ride in deep snow. The warmth of the furs eases my physical trial of the past days.

I see the house! Over Adampol, the Nazi flag waves high in the winter wind.

Mama and Tatek, encased in their desolation and despair, silently watch shadows lengthen on the library floor. It is so unlike the Christmases of the past, they must be thinking. Shattering the stillness, the door bangs against the wall as the pantry girl rushes in, tears streaming down her face. "Countess, they have come home, the little countesses are here. They're home!"

I race through the open door behind her, at first not registering the reflections on Mama's and Tatek's faces. Mama's is drawn and pale; Tatek's, bewildered.

"Christine, where is Basia?" asks Mama.

"Oh, she is still climbing out of the cart."

"And the boys?"

"Oh, don't worry, Mama, they are all right. The Russians have caught them."

I am so overwhelmed at being back at Adampol that

I feel no concern at all. I assume that the boys will come home sometime, just as Basia and I are home now.

Mama and Tatek, having some understanding of capture by the Russians, are horrified. Mama whispers, defiantly, "No, Tatek, no, not the Russians."

Why do they worry so? I am home!

THE OCCUPATION, 1939–1942, ADAMPOL
January 1940

The day is cold. Last night's snow and wind have left the trees bent under white drifts. Mama, peering out the frosted window, is prodded by restlessness, for she feels confined, restricted. We live in such a small part of the house; the Germans have commandeered all but a few rooms.

Jerome, Andrew, and Wladek were released by the Russians and escaped home through the German zone the same way we did. Now they spend most of their time outside, working with Tatek, managing the estate as ordered by the Germans. Today, because of the storm, we all are within these few rooms. Mama chooses to walk. Bundled in fur coats and felt boots, she and I set out, not from the main entrance to the house claimed by the Germans, but from the servants' entrance, which is now ours.

The sheath of ice on the kitchen steps is treacherous, so we hold on to each other for balance. My concentration on this maneuver is broken by a German soldier. He politely greets us; I stop and look up at him. He is young, blond, appealing. Mama quietly but firmly pushes me forward over the ice.

"Mama, I want to reply to him."

"No. Go ahead."

"But Mama. . . ."

While we walk briskly between the white raised edges of frozen road, I watch the dogs burrow freely back and forth through the snow. . . .

"Why didn't you let me speak with the German?"

"Because I do not want you to have anything to do with them."

"What do you mean, 'them'? I wanted to say something, only to that one."

"This time I will not argue with you, Christine. You are not to speak with German soldiers."

"But Mama, I don't want to speak with German soldiers. I want to say a few words to one."

"You must realize that they are *all* our enemies."

"What about the Germans who found me in the snow and the doctor who looked—"

"Christine, you must not see them as individuals. They are Germans, and *you* are not to speak with them."

It is of no use with Mama. There is only one way to behave, and that is as she has been instructing me since I was very small: "No, Christine, you are not to display your emotions and you should keep your moods to yourself."

I remember her sending Jerome away from the table because he was in an ugly humor.

"Go to your room, Jerome. Bad moods are private. When your mood has passed, then you may come back."

Mama may behave that way if she wishes, but I will behave as I please. I am determined to speak to the German soldier, to discover for myself if he is good or bad.

From my window I watch him, his blond hair glistening in the wind.

I watch Alisia. I have seen her standing by the piano while one of the Germans plays. She smiles at him while she praises the beauty of his melodic touch. She too plays the piano very well.

"Mama, why don't you mind when Alisia talks with the Germans?"

"She is an adult, and you are not; that is why."

Several days later I again walk along the road, this time by myself. When I meet the same German soldier, I stop.

"What is your name?"

"Ludwig. And yours, Countess?"

"Christine. How old are you?"

"Twenty-two, and you?"

"Sixteen."

"You are a pretty girl. It is too bad that we meet like this. I would like to meet you under different circumstances."

He pulls out a pack of cigarettes and offers me one. I take it. We walk along for a while in silence.

"Why?"

"Why what, Countess?"

"Why would you like to meet me under different circumstances?"

He throws me a little smile, but his face turns quickly serious.

"Well, because I—or rather we—really don't belong here; but you know what it is when you are drafted . . . you have to go."

"Couldn't you have refused, said that you didn't want to fight?"

"Of course not."

"Are you happy?"

"No."

"But you are glad that you won the war with Poland. . . ."

"No, I hate the war. I oppose it."

"Did you ever kill anyone?"

"No, not yet. I hope I don't have to. At home, I was attending a university to become a lawyer, so I was assigned to direct the HQ office."

"Why are you not an officer?"

"Well, I suppose that I am not really good material for an officer. I hold a rather mediocre post in the Army and I didn't join the Nazi party."

"Do you hate the Polish people?"

"Hate?" He paused. "Why should I, and for what reason? They fight for what is theirs. I don't hate them, I respect them."

"And the Russians . . . do you hate them?"

"No, as I told you, I don't hate anyone . . . only the war."

"How do you think all this will end?"

"I don't know, but I am sure it will not be a happy ending for us."

"Are you afraid?"

"Indifferent."

"Indifferent?"

"Yes, I really don't care. I want it finished, quickly."

"Finished, even at the cost of German defeat?"

"Even more so, at the cost of German defeat. We have no right to occupy other countries, and the end of the war means the return of freedom to all whom we now oppress."

Mama is wrong. Ludwig is a decent human being, in spite of the uniform he wears. It would be nice to meet under different circumstances.

"And you, Countess, do you hate us Germans?"

"I don't hate *you*, but I am not sure that all Germans are like you."

"Yes, of course, you are only sixteen, but you are growing up. Someday you will learn to hate us."

"I can't hate you, but I could never really be friends with you. I would be ashamed. . . ."

"Do you feel ashamed talking to me now?"

"No, but we are quite alone. Shame occurs only if others see and judge your actions."

"Would you meet me in a public place or restaurant?"

"I never would. I would be ostracized by all of the Polish people who know me."

For a time we are silent. Ludwig looks distant, then speaks wistfully.

"It is unfortunate. We are both young. Society dictates that we are to be enemies, to hate one another. Maybe someday, sometime when this is all over, you *would* meet me. Perhaps you could consider that. I do believe that someday we will lose this war and we won't be here. . . . Then you wouldn't be ashamed if we met, would you?"

I look him straight in the eye.

"I don't know. . . ."

February 1941

The German Army has taken a Polish prisoner, a boy, only seventeen. He is tied to a stake in the courtyard, where a bitter wind swirls the snow around him. The quadrangle is the site of one of the many "alterations" the Germans have made at Adampol. It is here that prisoners are "staked" prior to their execution. From the window of the dining room, Mama involuntarily notes the shivering figure. This prisoner, this Polish youth, could have been Andrew or Jerome, she muses. "What can he possibly have done that would cause them to leave him there so long?"

The wind increases during the night, the temperature drops, and there is more snow. In the morning, Mama finds that he is still there in the courtyard and wonders if he might not be dead. No. He shifts his head from side to side, then shuffles a foot . . . so alone.

"I am going to take him some soup," she announces.

Tatek rejoins, "They won't allow it."

"That is their concern. He has been there too long. Someone must give him something."

"You won't be permitted to go near him. No one can!"
I hear them continue their arguing.

"I cannot stand it any longer. He might have been my son."

"If you insist, I will take him some soup, but they are likely—"

"No, Tatek, I will take him the soup. A woman has a better chance."

Tatek shakes his head and mutters something, while Mama noisily dishes the soup. All of us hear her proceed, deliberately, down the servants' stairs, carrying the bowl of soup. The second she steps into the courtyard, a German corporal shouts, "*Halt!* Where do you think you are going?"

Mama pulls herself up straight and tall, then motions toward the Polish boy tied to the stake.

"Countess, you may go no farther!"

Stretching even taller, Mama shoves the bowl of soup into the hands of the startled German corporal. In a voice clear and controlled, she informs him, "I had no intention of going farther. You are going to take that boy this soup."

Astonished, the guard accepts the bowl, then carries it to the prisoner's stake. He holds the soup for the youth to drink. When he returns to his post, the bowl is empty.

October 1941

Mama now spends many hours sitting quietly in her chair by the library window, deep in reflection. Her shoulders are slightly bent and her hair is newly grayed; her eyes, always spirited, have not dulled.

Franus, our butler, has just entered the dining room to bring my parents a message from the general and his staff.

"The general wishes both of you to dine tonight with him and his officers, to celebrate the great success the Germans are having on the Russian front."

In mid-June of 1941, the Germans broke their agreement with the Russians and declared war against them. The border between the two countries was only seven miles from our home, so we were witness to the first German victories. Seldom facing any opposition from the Russians, the Germans proceeded as rapidly as their tanks could move.

Franus continues, "Countess, they ask you to dinner, but they want you to serve them and, if possible, to use what remains of our best china and silver."

Andrew sneers. "Give them potatoes on tin plates from the workers' kitchen. Nothing more."

"No," says Franus, "we cannot do it. A joke of this kind could make them very angry, and they are bad enough when they are kind."

"But what about the food?" Mama asks.

"Oh, they will provide all that is needed. They merely want your company at the table in your dining room, and a beautifully set table with all your best silver."

The sarcastic tone of Franus' voice registers his dislike of delivering such a message for Germans, whom he scorns.

Tatek looks at Mama quizzically. "Ah, now they want to steal our peace."

We have become used to rude interruptions and to degrading orders. There has been no single moment of privacy in our home for more than two years. We must continually circumvent their challenges. Mama resolves the dilemma.

"Tonight, I will have dinner with the general. The rest of you will not attend. And Franus will serve us and act as interpreter." Mama spoke no German.

She and Tatek both realize that at least one person must appear, and the fact that more do not will make the point.

The silver and china are placed on the table, as ordered. When it is time for dinner, Mama meets the general, who escorts her to the dining room. She places him at one end of the table, herself at the other. Six German officers are seated on each side; all of them are young and all are being sent to the front. The general rises to offer his toast.

"Countess, we are delighted with the accommodations at Adampol and indebted to you and the count for the careful way that you have managed the estate for us. We will be leaving for the Russian front tomorrow and we wish to express our appreciation to . . ."

He drones on and on about the fatherland and what they are setting out to accomplish. Mama half listens, knowing that as soon as he has finished his extended toast, and the ring of clinked glasses has subsided, she will be expected to respond.

With slow, conscious dignity she pauses to look each German officer squarely in the eye, to rest on each face long enough to cause a moment of uncertainty and a feeling of discomfort.

As her eyes focus at last on the general, seated at the opposite end of the long table, she is mindful of other guests who over so many years have been at this table. The china belonged to the Lubomirski estate at Kruszyna, and the silver was used by the Zamoyskis for three generations. Some wonderful people have touched them, and their spirits seem present as she now makes her own salute. Franus translates.

"General, officers, I hope, for the sake of your mothers, that you will come home safely."

She does not speak another word during the dinner.

January 1942

The sixth hour of 1942 I am lying in bed, half expecting the music to begin. There is none. Every year when I was a little girl, I was wakened on New Year's morning by a Jewish band from the village. They would come and play their two violins, trumpet, and accordion, as if to rouse us after the long celebrations of the previous night. This was a time to share a bit of money and food with people who were less fortunate.

Numerous rumors circulate in Poland about what is happening to the Jewish people. Mama and Tatek talk often about the Russians, who systematically execute the intelligentsia and the aristocracy, while the Germans execute the Jews or send them to concentration camps.

The only Jew I really know is my teacher, Mrs. Gurewicz. The Gurewiczes, who both were teachers in the village, came to the estate shortly after the German invasion. Mr. Gurewicz pleaded with my parents for help because his wife was Jewish. It was decided that they should stay on as teachers for the children.

Although we have been told that under no condition must we ever mention to anyone that Mrs. Gurewicz is Jewish, it is hard to believe that some of the Germans do not already know. As I think about her, with her dimpled cheeks and wide brown eyes, it seems impossible that the Germans would send her to a concentration camp. Yet Mama and Tatek say that if the Germans find her out, she will go.

THE NAZI RATE OF EXCHANGE

For the killing at Waeer, Poland, December 25, 1940, of a high German S.S. (police) official, the Nazis condemned to death every male, and by a later reprieve actually shot every fifth male in the village. An elderly man named Doctor W. B. Starski, who was lucky in the lottery that selected the victims for that mass killing, later escaped and brought the story to the United States. In this case the rate of exchange was 167 to one.

U.S. News & World Report, *July 3, 1942*

ADAMPOL 1942, NO MORE MEMORIES

As I sit on the bench in front of Adampol, the command that does not cease to reverberate is loud, cruel, and unqualified.

"You have two days to get out. You are to take nothing. Each room will be sealed."

"Hah!"

It is only Basia, her eyes swollen and red. I do not know how long I have been sitting here, amid the avalanche of memories. In a rare gesture of warmth, I pull her down beside me on the bench and put my arm around her shoulder.

"What shall we do?"

Basia tries to convince herself: "They can't throw us out. They can't do it!"

"What do you mean, they can't do it? They can and they are. We must face it. In two days we won't be here. Perhaps someday they will be defeated and pay a worse price."

For a while we are silent. I look up at the sky. "On whose side are You?"

"What did you say?" asks Basia.

"Oh, nothing. Basia, let's not sit here. Shall we go for a walk around the house? Anything is better than sitting here."

"No," she says, wiping away tears with her fist. "What do you think about opening all the cages, so that the pet animals can escape?"

The idea is a game for Basia, who is now thirteen. For me, it is the first act of planned defiance against an enemy I am old enough to understand and to hate. They will not hesitate to kill us if we are caught.

"All right, Basia, we will free the animals. At least the Germans will not have them."

We walk through the woods to avoid being seen from the road. Protected by branches and bushes, we scan all directions for Germans. Not seeing any, we run breathlessly toward the animal cage, where Jerome stands, gazing intently up at the trees. I touch his arm. He turns abruptly.

"Oh, it is you. God help me if they had caught me letting the owl out."

Basia and I burst into laughter.

"We had the same idea!"

I look at the open cage and then up to the top of the tree. The owl, as he surveys his new view of the world, is no longer attached to his perch and never again will serve as a decoy for hawks and kites amid shotguns cocked and ready. I leave Jerome and Basia and run to the barn to get some burlap bags. Then I hurry to the rabbit hutches, where I collect all of my friends.

Taking them one by one, I put them in the bags, with tears running down my cheeks. I kiss each one and whisper words of love and sorrow. The last one is Napoleon. All white with pink eyes, nose, and ears; he is my favorite. So many nights I smuggled him into my room and kept him in my bed with me all night. He was not housebroken and often the sheets had to be changed the next morning. But my maid was my friend, so while she would scold me, she would not get me in trouble by telling my mother about it.

With a heavy heart I kiss him once more. "Goodbye and take care of yourself." The job finished, I throw the bags over my shoulders and rejoin Jerome and Basia. We decide to let them out at the end of the vegetable garden. We know that with all the cabbage, carrots, and lettuce there they will have plenty to eat. And in the garden they have a better chance to escape from foxes. So we open the bags and out come the rabbits. We shoo them off and they disappear under the leaves and bushes.

"Now let's have a cigarette," I say. Jerome pulls a small tobacco box out of his pocket and some toilet paper. We sit down, roll our own cigarettes, and begin smoking. The tobacco is a mixture of God only knows what, and smells awful, but we enjoy it all the same.

I guess I had my first secret cigarette when I was nine years old, thanks to my father. One evening, as I was with him hunting woodcocks, I asked him to let me try one puff. I just wanted to know what it tasted like. He not only refused, but became quite angry at my request. So that did it. Since then I have been smoking, and what's worse, smoking Father's cigarettes, which I used to steal from him with great proficiency.

"We are going to Krakow, to Aunt Krystyna and Uncle Stefan," Jerome says.

"But why? Why not to one of our relatives who still live on their estates? Why to that awful city? I hate cities."

"I will tell you why. There have been more and more arrests every day. The city is safer because it is easier to hide among crowds of people if they begin looking for us."

I know that what Jerome says is true, and I know that we must go there . . . but I don't like the idea.

Andrew and Alisia suddenly come upon us, demanding, "Where have you been? Tatek wants to see you right away."

"We let loose the rabbits and the owl," Basia whispers secretively.

"Good for you," Andrew says with approval. "Two things the damned Germans won't get."

"They won't get the chickens, either," Alisia adds bitterly. "I told the cook to kill them and fry them for supper. What the hell, we might as well have a last feast. I don't think those two Gestapo pigs had enough time to see and record everything; certainly they didn't count the chickens."

We enter the house and climb the stairs to the library, where Tatek is sitting at the table, his head in his hands. He is unaware that we have come until Basia hugs him. His eyes search our faces.

"We have only two days left. The day after tomorrow, in the morning, we must leave. It will be very difficult, very difficult. . . ."

His voice trails off to a whisper caught by a sob in his throat. I am alarmed, for I have never seen my father cry.

No. He straightens his back and shoulders, pulled upright by some inner demand, which gives strength to his voice. "We shall be allowed to take very little. The

Germans sealed each door and they will decide what we can take, so . . . do not argue with them. We will go to the village in one of the carts and then by train to Krakow. Enough talk. We will do what we must.

"Someone should go to Wlodawa and send a telegram to Mama."

"I will take my bicycle," volunteers Jerome.

"Good. Just say, 'Don't come back, we are coming to you.' "

Again footsteps intrude. The Nazis enter without knocking. We look at each other but do not move. What this time? They walk straight to Tatek; one carries the long hunting coat, made of homespun green wool and lined with gray wolf fur, that is my father's favorite. The Nazi holds the coat over his left arm as he gestures with his right.

"*Herr Graf*, we want you to decide which of us should have your fur coat. We both want it."

Jerome gasps. I cannot breathe. Tatek, very silent, methodically rubs his hands behind his back while he stoops forward as if contemplating his answer. He turns toward the Nazis with a slightly ironical smile.

"*Meine Herren*. I would think that the one of you who expects to go first to fight for the fatherland on the Russian front ought to have the coat. It is rather cold there."

That is the last thing that the Nazis want to hear. Furious, they turn and leave the room.

Tatek is the image of courage and dignity, a worthy descendant of our forefathers, who were known as far back as 1331 for their great patriotism. Our family is one of the oldest in Poland. Many of our forefathers had gained fame serving their country in war and peace. In the sixteenth century some attained the highest positions in the kingdom. John Zamoyski became secretary to the king, then first chancellor of the kingdom, and finally commander in chief of the king's army. Not only did he defend Poland from many outside perils, but he also built the town and fortress of Zamosc, one of the few places to resist the Swedish invasion in the seventeenth century. In the eighteenth century, my great-grandfather Andrew Zamoyski, scholar, writer, and statesman, first chancellor to the king, was one of the creators of the Polish constitution of May 3, 1791. In Poland, the one who held the position of castellan of Krakow, the highest dignitary after the king, had the title of count, which was inherited by his descendants. Some of my forefathers held that position. The title of prince was given the same way, and my mother inherited it from her forefathers, who also held high positions in the kingdom.

All four of us look up at Tatek with admiration. We are proud to be part of him, and proud of our roots.

Tatek too is pleased, if only for a moment.

"Come, we must begin. The Germans are waiting for us."

They supervise our packing, checking each item as we put it in our suitcases, then double-checking to be sure that we haven't hidden something. Herded from one room to another, we accept every insult, every loss.

My room is opposite the staircase, so I am the first to

pack. The others are ordered to wait in my room until I am finished. With the words "Surely you don't want my old clothes," I decide defiantly that I will take everything. I open the wooden wardrobe, grab all that is on the hangers, and throw it on the bed.

"Not so quick, *Fräulein.*"

The Gestapo officer uncovers a sweater-jacket that Babcia knit for me from homespun wool. Then, addressing the other one, he says, "This will fit my wife. She will look pretty. It is good quality."

Quietly I curse, "You bastard."

After pawing through my other clothes, he turns back to the wardrobe. Tossing my wooden sandals on the bed, he laughs. "You can take those." He then grabs my winter felt boots, my riding boots, and my ski boots.

"Where are your skis, *Fräulein?*"

"I don't know. They were stolen in 1939 when the war started."

He shrugs his shoulders, then opens every drawer of my desk. The drawers have my jewelry in them, none of it precious, but it is dear to me. Each piece was a gift and has its own memory. There are the lapis lazuli necklace, the amber beads, a few sterling bracelets, and an enamel pin. He slips all of them into his pocket. I close my suitcase.

I watch them take everything else from my room, even the old dolls that I used to bury in the forest cemetery. At one time, there was a whole wall of dolls given to me at Christmas and on my namesake days. I never played with them but assigned them a special purpose. Each represented one of my tutors, governesses, parents, grandparents, or other relatives, someone who had authority over me. If I was punished by any of those people, I would grab "their" doll from my room and go to my cemetery in the woods. There I buried the doll, covered the grave with forget-me-nots, and made a headstone. Later, when my anger subsided, I would dig up the doll and return it to my bedroom shelf. I once buried Babcia, my grandmother, and forgot. Only when she gave me a small diamond ring with two rubies at Christmas did I remember with fright that she was still in the cemetery, frozen beneath the snow. I wish, now, that I could bury the Nazis forever.

Instead of sealing my room, one of them points to me. "You can spend your last night here with your sister, one on the bed, one on the couch. Move to the next room."

Jerome's room, Andrew's room, and Alisia's are locked and sealed. Tatek is allowed to take one small object for Mama. He selects a bronze statue with a black marble pedestal, which for her has both sentimental and artistic value. The Nazis say no. It is too valuable. He then takes from her night table a small iron cross which has been in the family for over two hundred years. The German snatches it from his hand.

"Is this silver?"

"No, it is iron."

"You can have that crap."

Now we are confined to three rooms. The Gestapo, having sealed all the others, leave immediately for Wlodawa; they will be back in the morning to preside over our departure. It is a relief to have a few hours without their presence. We gather around a small table in the kitchen. The cook opens the oven. Yes, there are chickens, golden brown and smelling more wonderful than any chicken dinner I can remember. For three years our meals have been very simple, and seldom if ever have we had chicken, wonderful golden brown chicken.

"Who wants a drink?"

Tatek is holding a bottle of vodka.

"I do!" I had never had hard liquor before.

He pours a small amount into my glass, which disappears in one gulp.

"Slowly, now. You will be drunk."

"So what?"

Tatek obliges me with a little more. I again swallow it and hold out my empty glass. "Tatek, please?"

I begin to feel warm, my face burning. With another glass, I speak as if my mouth were full of noodles. I curse. The bad words, which I had never used before, are refined compared to the behavior of the Gestapo.

"I wish the S.O.B.s would rot in hell."

Andrew adds, "In hell? No, that is too late. Let them rot *now*."

"Dirty Krauts," Jerome contributes. "Bastards."

Tatek does not mind. He laughs with us. There are no words bad enough to describe our feelings. The words do not sound vulgar; they sound appropriate. The curse is our only weapon.

"Chickens, chickens, chickens," I repeat . . . as all begins to blur.

"Someday we will cut off the Germans' heads, like the chickens."

The voices seem to grow louder. I am so tired I cannot think, cannot find new words to compete with the other voices. . . .

(It didn't take more than a few minutes before I was completely drunk. I was told the next day that I laughed and cried throughout the whole dinner, praising the chickens and damning the Germans. It took quite an effort on the part of my father to keep me quiet and restrain me from going after the Germans.)

Oh! . . . my head. I can barely stand to move it. Twelve hours later, I try to recollect. Jerome meets me in the pantry, where we both settle down to breakfast. Neither of us speaks. He looks uncomfortable, so I suppose that his head also throbs. Finally he manages a smile and says, "I did not know that you possessed such a rich vocabulary. Congratulations."

I am pleased.

I leave the kitchen, a slice of bread still in my hand, to wander aimlessly.

I pass under the terrace and there I see Ludwig, the young German soldier whom I could not hate. He faces me, but does not smile. Then his eyes seek the ground.

"We are not a part of all this. We are not part of the Gestapo. I am sorry about what is happening to you. I would never do such a thing. I want to help. If I can in any way . . . ?"

I turn from him without answering, walk a few steps, and then turn back. I have learned. I now know how to hate. Pointing my finger directly at Ludwig I say, *"Sie sind nicht mehr als ein Deutsch!"* (You are nothing but a German!)

We are leaving Adampol. I carry my suitcase down the stairs and out to the waiting cart, where Jerome and Andrew stand with theirs. The servants cry as they shake hands with each of us. I will not cry. The Nazis are watching from an upstairs window, I know. I raise my head.

When we are all assembled there are seven on the cart with our baggage. Now we are gypsies, homeless aristocrats. I turn to look back at Adampol.

"I will never love a home again."

The road we travel passes through at least four kilometers of forest. When we are halfway, we hear a scurrying in the bushes and trees. Foresters, peasants with their children, who had not dared come to Adampol, to the house, now emerge from the dense woods. They embrace us, cry, say their final goodbye, first to Tatek and then to the rest of us one by one. I cannot hold back the tears any longer.

The train is crowded, hot, and there is nothing to eat, for the vendors who once passed from car to car are only a memory. Sixteen hours later it stops outside Krakow, pulling alongside another train on the adjoining track. I look out the window. What I see makes me shiver.

"My God, it is true."

Animal wagons, sealed and locked with iron bars and tiny slits like crated windows. Through the slits, pale and tired faces are looking out hopelessly. Outside the cars, German soldiers are standing on guard. I close the shade on my window and turn away.

"Tatek, Tatek . . ."

But my voice falls away. It is a transport of people for the concentration camp. I cannot help.

Looking at these people, I realize how little I have lost and how lucky I have been so far. War has not even touched me yet. What if these pale faces in the little windows were my parents' or my brother's or sister's?

As the train pulls into the Krakow station I again raise the curtain and look out.

"Mama! Tatek, Mama is there!"

I am the first off the train. I run and hold her, tears freely pouring from my eyes. As I hold my mother tight, I feel peace and courage returning to my heart.

Part Two

KRAKOW

POLAND, LAND OF THE WHITE EAGLE

During her century and a quarter of complete eclipse, when her next door neighbors, who had torn her to pieces, sought to smother her national character with rifles and soldiers, Krakow, ancient capital, kept alight the fierce flame of Poland's independence.

... a clarion call. A strange blending of taps and reveille, this bugle call rings out from the tallest of Saint Mary's twin towers. But why should its sweet notes be strangled so abruptly?

A student ... explains that the *hejnal* is a memorial to a trumpeter who, seven centuries ago, while calling the people to the defense of the city walls and encouraging them in the midst of battle with his stirring blasts, was shot to death by a Tatar arrow. The choked note was the bugler's farewell.

National Geographic, *April 1932*

AUGUST AND SEPTEMBER 1942

It was built in the late eighteenth century. The once gleaming white townhouse is elegant and graceful, with its high vaulted archway that gave the finest of horse-drawn carriages access to the cobblestoned courtyard.

My grandfather, Dziadzio, and his brothers and sisters lived in the house during the winter months while attending school in Krakow.

Now its entire ground floor is rented to other families. Uncle Stefan and Aunt Krystyna, the present owners, occupy the first floor along with far too many Zamoyskis and Lubomirskis, all of whom use a common kitchen, living room, and bathroom. My parents, Jerome, Andrew, Basia, and I have three tiny rooms, once servants' quarters. My room, approximately the size of a single bed, is surrounded by other rooms, also too small, containing too many. In desperation, I stare through an open pane in a window curtained with cobwebs, like a prisoner seeking fresh air.

I long for Adampol, for my clean, spacious room with its tapestry curtains and bedspread, its desk which originally belonged to Mama, and its bookcases stuffed with an ample family of dolls from my childhood. I long for the immensity of a home where I could roam for kilometers without leaving the estate, where I could settle securely in front of a great white marble fireplace that was twice my height. Mentally, I revisit one room and then another. As I look at the marble bust and the two great bronze urns resting on the grand mantel in the library, I realize that I took so many things for granted. I knew who I was then, and what I could claim.

Now, looking down upon this grimy courtyard, I feel lost, hopeless, confined to a stifling room in which I did not choose to live, amid a terrifying war in which I did not choose to fight. Here in Krakow we can claim nothing and have to scrap for everything, even for air to breathe, and we must hide everything, even our lost identities.

Tatek is hiding somewhere in the larger, more anonymous city of Warsaw. Several days after we arrived in Krakow he was warned by friends that the Gestapo knew he had hidden Jews at Adampol. Just as we hide clothes under the beds and radios behind clocks, we hide our words from everyone, except those closest to us.

A Jewish man named Scharff, too, is being hidden. His alias, to protect him, is Zygmund Durakowski. While I peer through my window, I see the short, plump gentleman with a full gray beard who has been living here since 1940, when Uncle Stefan and Aunt Krystyna befriended him. We are never permitted to call him anything but Uncle Durakowski. Of course I do not voice the many questions this "uncle" raises, yet while his life is being saved, his presence endangers the lives of all of us. Sometimes I am ashamed to even think this. The chimney smoke from Auschwitz, its stench of burned bodies carried east by the wind, makes it impossible for any creature living nearby to avoid recognizing the smell of death.

Aunt Krystyna's voice echoes from yesterday: "Christine, he was your grandfather's dear friend and he is ours. He has been very good to us. Why do you think he delivers those cigarette papers for your grandmother, Babcia, to fill with tobacco? Yes, he sells them and then gives Babcia the money so that she will feel she is contributing something to the life of the family. After Dziadzio died and his body lay here until burial, Uncle

Durakowski meekly asked if he might spend a few minutes alone with his old friend. I stood outside the door, while a voice, strong, yet choking with tears, intoned the Hebrew prayer for the dead."

I wonder how many Jews are in this house. We are all trapped guests who depend on Uncle Stefan's charity. We have made waiting our way of life.

It begins in the early morning with, first in line outside the bathroom door, Uncle Stefan standing and reading his German newspaper, thundering at its false propaganda. Aunt Krystyna, a singular exception, avoids waiting by rising before dawn, but her sons, Jas and Stas, eight and nine years old, stand behind their father, kicking and shoving each other. Blond, barefoot, in green-, yellow-, and red-striped underwear, they look like twins.

Behind them Aunt Erika knits while she waits; she still does not know whether her husband is alive or dead. Her Viennese origin is of great help against the Germans. Under her bed are cases of false documents, false I.D.s. She is a real fighter.

In a shimmering long silk robe, with beautifully arranged hair, Aunt Rose Lubomirska is a startling contrast to the rest of us in the early light. She didn't need to wait for the war to count her losses. Both her husband and a baby daughter died in the 1930s. Mama always defends her brother's wife by arguing that the tragedies of Rose's life have made her overly emotional. Certainly her involvements in crusades and causes often disturb other members of our family. This lonely woman's only solace are her two daughters. Natalia, her favorite, has thick dark hair and the face of a Greek statue. Her nightgown is far too short, as she is over six feet tall. Elizabeth, short and plump, is oppressively religious, and sure to become a nun. I avoid her, as she tells our parents about anything we do that deviates from the Ten Commandments.

As the day progresses, friends with no other occupation constantly overflow our one "large room." Some joke and play cards, but many merely sit and wait.

Others come with a different purpose. Uncle Stefan, who trades in the black market, buys valuables from the desperate who must sell to survive and then resells at a higher price. While ostensibly outlawing what is now the Poles' major source of income, the Germans are some of its best, if covert, customers.

I do wish that Tatek were here. We have heard nothing from him.

The idea of Tatek being hunted is hateful to me.

There was a time when we were the hunters. My father used to invite five or six guns, mostly friends and relations, to hunt wild boars. It was always in winter before or after Christmas, when the forest was white with snow, which made tracking easier. At dusk the hunters would be coming back, taking off their big felt boots on the wild boar's skin near the door and throwing off their coats and fur caps to sit in front of the fire, warming their hands and discussing all the events of the day. It was fun for us children to hear all the stories: their hairbreadth escapes from special wild boars, stories about hunting dogs and their names.

To my dying day, I will remember the moment when

Tatek told me that I could come to the big hunt the next day. I think it was my great-uncle who had pleaded my cause. Up till then we children were only allowed to go boar hunting when it was a private hunt, just Mama, Tatek, and Grandpa. Our forests were divided into fifty-hectare sections by forest roads which sometimes ran for kilometers in straight lines. Each forest guard had a number of those sections under his care. He had to supervise the replanting of parts that had been cut down the year before, police poachers, take care of the roads, and track game two or three times in winter when there was a hunting party.

That morning, I remember, I was up and dressed at an ungodly early-morning hour, and when I ran downstairs to the dining room the butler, Franus, was just beginning to do the room and lay the table for breakfast. I helped him, to pass time, which was dragging, as time drags when you are waiting for something wonderful to happen. About half-past seven Mama came down and went to the kitchen to supervise the preparing of sandwiches for everybody, guests and trackers. At last, one by one, our five guests came down for breakfast, while Father was outside talking to the trackers. They said we had wild boars in four sections, and there was a very large and clever tusker that even had a name, Micki, and had always managed to outwit everybody. So about nine A.M. two sleighs were waiting at the front door and we were all ready to start.

There were five guns, two uncles and three cousins. My father, being the host, did not have a gun, just his hunting knife. The sleighs were dismantled farm sleds covered with a sort of mattress, and you had to sit sideways with your feet dangling. It was easy to jump down, even when the horses were moving.

I sat between my father and my great-uncle, with my fur coat pockets bulging with packs of sandwiches my mother had had to force me to take, and which I was glad of later. The sun had come out, the sky was blue, no clouds and no wind. A deep silence reigned, as if the forest had fallen into a fairy sleep under a blanket of snow.

The other sleigh was following with six forest guards. Behind that came a third sleigh, which had only boards and was intended to carry the game.

Nobody felt like talking, and when someone did speak, it was in a hushed voice, as if in church. Then we came to a stop. One of the foresters came over, we turned to the right, the others did not follow.

And now as the horses walked slowly, Tatek touched my great-uncle's arm. Without a word, Uncle slipped down and stood behind a sort of screen made out of branches as we drove on. About a hundred and fifty meters farther it was the turn of the next hunter, and so we dropped them one by one, till at last only Tatek and I were left. A few hundred meters after the crossroad, we jumped down and watched the sleigh drive away and disappear at the next turning.

Tatek placed me just in front of him in the screen stand, so he could see over my head. He had told me earlier that, once in the stand, you must not move, so of

course I did my best. But when you are freezing, all sorts
of things seem to happen. My nose began to itch and I
was terrified I would sneeze.

Suddenly there came a very short bugle call. The
beaters had started. They walked in complete silence,
just breaking a twig from time to time. Something caught
my eye: a snow-white chickadee landed on a twig a few
inches from my head, like a white puff of cotton with
two shining black eyes. Suddenly my father squeezed
my arm. I froze and tried to catch a sound that would
tell me where to look. Then, like a ghost, a few yards
away a silver-gray shape slipped noiselessly from behind
a snow-covered fir tree. I could see the tusks, and I knew
it was Micki. He had fooled us once more. As he stood
there halfway out of the bushes observing the road, two
shots rang out and with one bound Micki was across the
road and disappeared in the forest.

I looked at Tatek. He was smiling, and I knew he was
glad that Micki was safe.

"Don't let's wait for the horses. Come, we will see
who has been shooting," he said. At the crossroad, the
sleigh caught up with us. The hunters had already left
their stands and were grouped together, talking.

"Well," said Tatek, "what's going on?"

"I don't know," answered my cousin. "There must
have been about ten of them. The sow was leading, so
of course I did not shoot, I was waiting for the boar at
the end. So I shot the last one, but it wasn't a tusker."

"Come, let's see," said Tatek, as he bent down to
inspect the tracks. "One bullet ripped a tree, but here is
a drop of blood. Let's have the dog."

Adampol. The interior courtyard showing the guest house wing and the entrance to the chapel.

Adampol. Entrance hall of the main house. Wild boar skins cover the floor and buckhorn trophies line the walls. The big hat table was carved by an Adampol carpenter. After a big hunt party, vodka and snacks were served on it before dinner. Murals of my father's old castle Rozanka, high on the walls, were painted by Count Zenon Brzozowski.

Adampol. The library. The pair of lions by the hearth were a wedding present to my mother from her uncle. On the table, the statue "Two Winds" is by a famous Polish sculptor.

Adampol. The hothouse. The palm tree, a gift from Czar Alexander III, stands in a bed of colorful mosses arranged in a mosaic by Mazur, our gardener. Canary birds lived and nested here.

Adampol. Large stair hall off the entrance hall where our Christmas tree stood during the holidays.

Kruszyna, the fourteenth-century "Rosary" castle of my mother's family.

Dziadzio, my maternal grandfather,
Prince Stefan Lubomirski.

My parents, Count Constantine Zamoyski and Princess Nathalie Lubomirska, at Kruszyna on their wedding day, June 4, 1921.

My mother and her sister, Aunt Krystyna Lubomirska, 1920.

My most beloved uncle, Prince
Stefan Lubomirski.

Mama at a costume ball at
Kruszyna, 1918, dressed as a
page at the court of bygone
Polish kings.

The Czar's borzois at Kruszyna which Mama
saved: Pytat, Tea, Bey, Kidyin, and Pasza.

Myself, age 3, in front of my parents'
town house on Aleja Röz
12, in Warsaw (1929).

Myself and my brother Jerome at Adampol, 1927.

The dog was on the sleigh, a cocker spaniel who during his sixteen years had tracked about a hundred wounded wild boars. His name was also Micki. My father whistled and Micki came like a shot, picked up the trail, and disappeared. A moment later we heard him barking, and by his voice we knew the wild boar was dead.

The beaters had come out by now, and the other sleighs were there too. The wild boar was carried out of the bushes and tied to the boards. Tatek broke an oak twig with some dry leaves, dipped it in the bullet hole in the boar, and offered it on his hunting knife to my cousin, who accepted it with a warm thank you and stuck it in his fur cap.

Then we started for the next section of the forest. It was already noon, and I was hungry, but my pride as a hunter would not allow me to be the first to eat. So I put my hand into my pocket, managed to make a hole in the sandwich wrap, and broke off a tiny bit, which I slipped in my mouth.

No use; my great-uncle saw it.

"That's a good idea, let's look at those sandwiches. I'd rather carry them in my stomach than in my pocket." He laughed, and that settled the matter. How we all enjoyed it.

We had three more places to go, all far apart, and by four o'clock it was getting dark. Still, we brought back four wild boars, but Micki was not among them.

That hunting party lasted three days, and it was the last one.

Now we were the game that the Germans hunted.

■ ■ ■

The days, weeks, another month pass. Mama will not tolerate my lassitude and spoke to Basia and me last night.

"It is time that the two of you return to school."

"But Mama, you have seen the German posters plastered everywhere in this city. For us school is forbidden. We are likely to be arrested and sent to labor camps in Germany."

"Yes, I know, but the effect of being without instruction is more dangerous. I have found an excellent secret school which you can attend safely."

"Why won't you listen? Why bother trying to do anything? I see no purpose in it when the Germans only want us for manual labor."

"Faith, Christine, you must have faith and believe that someday you will be free again. Then you will need your education. We shall enroll you tomorrow."

That was that!

Mama has placed me in another convent school. One of the best preparatory schools in Poland prior to the war, nuns maintain its original excellence in what is officially a cooking school. So we attend class in a large kitchen where potatoes, mushrooms, cabbage heads, and cookbooks are spread over the tables, while large pots of water boil on the woodstove.

I did not expect this to be so agreeable. The other girls are not silly and aloof, as I had anticipated, but open and generous.

It is true that this retaliation against German rules definitely alters my attitude. I even respect the nuns, their willingness to risk so much, their courage. At each entrance to the building a nun stands guard, while others are posted at various points in the corridors so that in the event of a German visit they could pass word, one to another, like a living telephone line. That way our notes and textbooks would be concealed in a wall vault behind the painting of the Madonna before the Germans reach us. They would only find a cooking class in progress. That, of course, is quite legal.

There is an uneasy balance between the requirements of my studies at the cooking school and the realities imposed by German food rationing. Much of my life is spent standing in queues, hoping hour after hour that a certain needed item rumored available in an official store (designated for Poles) will still be in supply.

Our search for food, both legal and illegal, becomes our way of survival. Official food ration cards provide us at best with a starvation menu of moldy black bread, made from flour stretched with sawdust; beet marmalade, with its distinctive bittersweet flavor of soil; gray tough noodles; and suet, our only source of fat. "Coffee," brewed from rye and acorns, is the German invention, "ersatz." We have none of these delicacies in quantities sufficient to feed a mouse, so we must find illegal food. The pursuit is dangerous and the price exorbitant.

At night I listen to the people in the front room with Uncle Stefan as they talk about the latest bit of food and how it entered the city. With chunks of meat under skirts, sausages wrapped around waists, and carrying double-bottomed baskets filled with eggs but covered with flowers, women accomplish most of the smuggling.

Farm products, except for a few vegetables, and all livestock must be registered with German authorities and delivered to them at the time of harvest or butchering. Peasants are entitled to keep enough to insure their own slow starvation. Disobeying the law results in extreme penalties—a risk sometimes compensated by a large profit, so peasants continue to feed the city. They successfully raise chickens, pigs, and cattle in cellars or in newly dug underground tunnels, only to face search patrols at the city outskirts, in railroad stations, or on small back roads. But we Poles are stubborn. We have the wit and courage to succeed.

Our family has little money for black market food. Mama sets aside a small portion of what she earns secretly tutoring a doctor's children in French and English for "significant extras."

It is Sunday. Jerome and I sit on my bed peering at the soup plates on our laps. Among thick noodles, carrots, and potatoes swims a white, peculiarly shaped ingredient. Gingerly I taste it. "Ah, sliced udders."

Jerome burps.

"Don't be so touchy. It could be worse. Tits provide protein like any other meat."

"And milk at the same time," he adds sarcastically.

"And by the way, did you hear the story about the man smuggling the cow's udder?"

"Tell me!"

"As the train was nearing the city, a guarded whisper spread through the crowds: *Attention*, raid. Everyone hastily hid their smuggled goods under benches, in glass lampshades, wherever there was space. A young man, immobilized by the crowded corridor, could not find a hiding place for the cow's udder in his bag. He managed to squeeze the udder into his trousers, but unfortunately, when the trousers burst a button, one of the tits slipped out.

"An embarrassed woman called it to his attention. As he tried to push it inside, it kept slipping out, so finally he took out his pocket knife and cut it off. The woman fainted."

We both laugh so hard that we nearly spill the rest of the soup. It feels wonderful to truly laugh again, but our thoughts inevitably revert to our work passes. In Krakow, we, like every Pole over seventeen, must obtain an I.D. card, called a *Kriegsgewichtig*, officially approved by the Germans, to certify employment in either a war industry or one that contributes to it. Without such a card we constantly risk being shipped to Germany for factory labor.

Police stop people at random to check their work passes. They close entire city blocks without warning, make a dragnet, and haul all able-bodied unemployed out of their houses. Jerome and I have good cause to worry.

The family gathers to discuss our predicament, as they do for all important issues. Mama, Uncle Stefan, Aunt Krystyna, Cousin Natalia, Jerome, and I review the options. Men are considered both better laborers and more likely to be involved in subversive activities, so Jerome is in the gravest danger. Being so tall and powerfully built, he is conspicuous in any crowd, the perfect target for a dragnet. Uncle Stefan suggests, "I think perhaps I can arrange a job for you in a cement factory just outside Krakow, where Herr Klaus, a friend, is the head director. You know he is a *Volksdeutscher* [a Pole of German nationality because of German parentage]."

"But what would I do there, Uncle Stefan?"

"There is a chance you might not even have to appear for work. It is the I.D. card that is important. Herr Klaus is a kind man, and has saved a number of Poles from deportation by giving them employment. I know him well, but—we should go as soon as possible, yes, first thing tomorrow."

When Jerome's dilemma seems settled for the moment, it is my turn. Cousin Natalia asks, "Christine, you remember the doctor to whom I took you when you had just come from Adampol with the nasty flu? I am sure he could place you at the city hospital. You would be well protected with a position there, because the Germans still consider hospitals important, even Polish hospitals."

Mama seems pleased.

"Yes, Christine, I think it is a splendid idea. If you like the work, you might even one day make a career of it."

"But I don't know anything about hospitals."

Natalia laughs. "Oh, you will learn. They might even make a nurse out of you."

On our way there the next day, Natalia whispers, "Promise, Christine, you will never repeat what I tell you."

I promise but am puzzled by the secrecy.

"Listen carefully, and don't ask any questions. Because he has many contacts with the Germans and therefore knows a great deal about how their operations work in this city, Dr. Mazur can be very helpful. He is able to provide I.D. cards, but also to discover proposed arrests in advance, to warn potential victims so that they can escape and—"

"How can he do this?"

"I told you: Don't ask questions!"

But I do ask, only one. "Will I be able to manage a hospital job?"

As we enter his office, Dr. Mazur, in a big leather chair, is bending over his desk. He is a short, funny-looking man. His hair, thick and blond, is parted in the middle and rises like a crest above his freckled face. Triangles of pink skin pop out between his shirt buttons. His bright blue eyes peer at me through horn-rimmed glasses.

"Nice to see you again. I hope it is not your flu that brings you back. How do you feel?"

"No, Doctor, it is not the flu, although I still ache and cough a great deal. I have a different problem this time."

Natalia interrupts. "She needs an I.D. She is over seventeen and in danger without a *Kennkarte*."

He smiles, then turns to me. "Tell me, what are you trained for?"

"I have never worked, but I can learn."

"Some experience would make it much easier."

"I think an occupation in a hospital is very rewarding; that in itself would give me initiative," I answer, trying to sound positive. In truth, I think I would faint or throw up if left with a patient half dead from bloody wounds, but there is no alternative.

"Don't worry, I will see what I can do. Perhaps you might work as a nurse's aide; then little by little we could train you. We have a fine nursing program at the hospital—forbidden, of course." While I envision dirty bedpans, smelly wounds, and needles with blood, Dr. Mazur continues, earnest wrinkles on his forehead. "Remember not to talk to anyone about our training; never, under any circumstance, say a word about it! Your German I.D. card will indicate you are a nurse; that will cover you, and the rest we will take one step at a time."

When I thank him, promising not to divulge anything, he suggests I go along home, as he wants to talk with Natalia.

"Christine, the best thing for butterflies in the stomach is hot soup."

Mama is right. She and I are still talking when Natalia, opening the door, announces triumphantly, "You are to see him next Monday at the city hospital."

OCTOBER AND NOVEMBER 1942

In fall, the cold wind finds its way into every unprotected corner of this city. Sometimes I stuff the sleeves and front of my flimsy clothes with newspapers, but in the rain, which makes the newsprint come off on my arms and neck, I shiver.

Today I am warm. Aunt Erika made a lining for my coat from a woolen blanket obtained through the black market. Silently thanking my favorite aunt, I pull it tight around me as I walk.

On my first day of work at the hospital, I confront the large gray building with misgivings, then tell myself that even as a little girl I could never resist a challenge, nor could I allow anyone or anything to taunt me into admitting failure. I pull open the heavy steel door and with an air of confidence enter the hall, an emergency room, filled with sick and wounded on stretchers. Moans, then screams, emanate from the shadows beside me. A face is twisted with pain, yet the enormous woman carries no visible sign of wounds. One of the two men who wheel her away leans over to comfort her.

"In just a few moments you will have your baby and it will all be over."

I resolve never to have a child.

Dim light, filtered through small gray windows, exposes the gray stone floors littered with papers and blood-soaked bandages. Pails of refuse give off a foul odor. I cannot look. Someone bumps into me and yells, *"Move!"*

The man on the stretcher being whisked by me is grotesquely mangled. While the room spins, I sink to a bench to regain my balance.

"Ah, Christine, you are ready to begin."

Dr. Mazur touches my shoulder, so I try to stand.

"Good, here is your identification card."

He hands me a document. Then, putting his arm around my shoulder, he asks me to meet Ella in his office.

"Now, Ella, I want you to give Christine a white gown and show her around the emergency room, so to acquaint her with our work here."

"Sure, Doctor, I'll be glad to do it."

"You will make a fine nurse someday," says Ella. "I am a good judge of character. Do you enjoy the prospect of being a nurse? Of course you do. I don't need to ask, I can tell."

While she asks and answers all her own questions and I attempt to cover my disgust and anxiety with a smile, we go to the laundry room, where I try on gowns. All are too small, so I ignore my ridiculous appearance and squeeze into one of them.

"There," says Ella. "A nurse if I ever saw one!"

Walking down the hallway, Ella briefs me about each door and closet, as well as every doctor and nurse. Actually, I enjoy her droll intermingling of fact and gossip, for it alleviates my distress at being here.

Genuine coffee and cake. These are the rewards she offers when we return to Dr. Mazur's office.

"Ella, where did you find such excellent cake? It must be made with real butter."

"I made it. Peasants who come here for treatment often pay with farm produce instead of money: white flour, eggs, butter, and sugar stolen from the Germans. You will gain a lot from me. Just stay around."

Maybe, with the prospect of good food, this won't be so bad after all.

Ella assigns me the least demanding tasks. I roll bandages, wash instruments; she sterilizes them, sets up trays for the doctors. And so we work side by side through the afternoon. I want to be Ella's friend, to believe that I can trust her and that she will understand, no matter what. Before I tell her my secrets, I should know her better, I admonish myself. But then I wonder if she will always be here to listen to me. Ever since I lost Adampol, I have craved a friend.

We have been coworkers only a few days, but already I talk without reserve. I repeatedly recount my loss of Adampol, for I still am unable to accept my present life. Ella listens to my litany but does not comprehend it. When I describe my home in detail, cataloguing all that I most miss, she seems amazed. I tell her how fortunate she is to have lost so little; she responds with silence. Once she said, "Well, I suppose if my family had been your family's servants and we, too, had been thrown out with you, then I might slightly understand."

Ella's father is a postal clerk. Her mother works hard caring for the eight children and their small apartment in a poor section of Krakow. Ella is proud of the fact that the apartment is near the hospital, so she does not have to travel far to work, but she never invites me there. Why does she emphasize that it is too simple, too humble, for a Zamoyski?

"A home," she says, "is four or eight walls, painted clean or dirty gray, a bed to sleep on, a kitchen stove to cook on. That is all."

Heritage, tradition, family pride—these are concepts she will not consider.

Ella talks continually about her boyfriends, always in the plural. With no experience, I cannot judge the truth of her stories. She is different from the people I have known, without the same upbringing. When we eat together, she picks her teeth with her fingers, burps, and uses crude words. And she finds a sexual connotation in everything I say. Even though her behavior is so different, I am attracted to her, for there is much I want to learn from her.

I have thought of myself as polished, well brought up, cultured; yet Ella, so clever and quick, is the one who knows how to get what she wants. Always cheerful, she never seems to be frightened, even when I know that she is.

CHRISTMAS 1942

It is almost Christmas, the first in my life not spent at Adampol, and I am in a black mood. Tatek still must be hiding in Warsaw. Today, December eighteenth, Dr. Mazur asks me to come to his office immediately. I have

worked hard and can't imagine what I have done wrong.
When I open his door, the doctor surprises me.

"Christine, how good to see you. You are doing very
well here. There are two things we must discuss—"

Bursting in without knocking, Ella demands, "Well,
is she one of us?"

Bewildered, I ask, "Oh, should I leave?"

"No, stay." Dr. Mazur's keen eyes search my own.

"Christine, we would like you to join the underground.
We need a person who speaks both French and English."
Without waiting for my answer, he announces, "Also,
you shall begin nurse's training in January."

I am speechless. My pride at being asked, at seventeen,
to serve my country overwhelms my fear that I will be
caught. In spite of the danger, I do want to try, but with
school, hospital work, and standing in queues for food . . .

"Dr. Mazur, you are needed in emergency, *immediately*!"

"I will be back shortly. In the meantime, you must
decide," Dr. Mazur says as he leaves.

Ella, still grinning, makes herself comfortable in the
doctor's chair.

"Of course you want to be in the underground. Don't
be afraid, you will be assigned to me, so we will be
together. Will you join?"

"Yes—but I didn't expect this. I don't know if I can
manage. Do you know what I mean?"

"Of course I do!"

I am not sure she does at all. She always claims to
understand but never really seems aware of the specific

problem. Sometimes Ella's all-embracing enthusiasm makes me angry.

She reproaches me. "You look so troubled, as if you were alone in this. No matter what happens, we will win in the end. Dr. Mazur plans to assign you to help Allied soldiers because you speak English and can talk to them. There are several in this area, prisoners of war who have managed to escape from German camps."

"But Ella, surely I cannot help just by talking or keeping them company."

"That too, but your most important job will be hiding them, providing food, clothes, and in some cases false documents so that they will be able to move about."

"I can't find clothes and food for myself. I don't know this city well."

"Oh, you will learn in no time," she assures me. "And besides, you may even find a handsome Englishman and fall in love with him."

"In love? Not me. I think love brings a lot of trouble."

"Trouble?" she exclaims, jumping out of the doctor's chair. "It's wonderful. If you tried it, you would find it is anything but trouble. Really, have you never been in love?"

"No. Only puppy love: Cousin Andrew."

Waving a large piece of gauze, Ella dances around the room and, swooping over, places it on my head as she begins to sing the wedding march.

"Ella, you are crazy."

She won't stop laughing and singing. Finally I interject, "And you—have you been in love?"

"Me? Of course. I am in love almost every other day."

"Just for once, be serious."

To diminish the potential consequences, Ella is making my joining the underground an occasion for a party. How important to them am I, really?

While she clowns, I search for the answer, knowing I will not say no, yet not sure I want to say yes. If I do join the underground I will be imprisoned by it. I will never be free to leave if I don't like it. And do I have the right to jeopardize my entire family? They didn't ask me about Uncle Durakowski, I admit. We all are doomed by the Germans, and perhaps I have a better chance of surviving by remaining inconspicuous, hoping for a miracle. But I hate the Germans more than I fear them, and here is opportunity to act, to fight back. How can I say no?

Dr. Mazur reappears, looks quizzically at Ella.

"Have you convinced Christine?"

"She didn't need much convincing."

"Good. Then, Christine, you are ready to take the oath. You will be an official member of the Polish Underground Army!"

I feel the blood rushing to my head. Saying yes to Ella was one thing, but now, the oath, so soon? Dr. Mazur asks me to raise my right hand. I hear my own voice repeating words: a solemn promise to defend my country even at the risk of my life, a pledge of secrecy.

They congratulate me and produce three glasses. We raise a toast in celebration. Soon I feel very pleased, and for a few hours we inhabit a world that does not exist.

Once home, I go straight to my room, while my head spins thoughts and dreams.

I am a heroine. A trainload of German soldiers and supplies has been blown up, a feat of incredible courage. Underground officers everywhere drink to my bravery. A bridge explodes, killing a high-ranking German general. I am an officer in the underground. Young men seek my company, for I am a leader in a mighty army that is overthrowing the Germans. Then, amid waving flags, I ride in an open car while thousands of people lining the streets shout my name. Honor, fame. I am back in Adampol. I am drunk.

It must be morning; I roll over in bed, holding my throbbing head. Slowly the memory of yesterday's commitment . . . What in hell did I do? The Germans execute members of the underground, shoot them without asking questions. I start to shake. If I am caught, they will kill my family as well. I am not at all courageous, and given the opportunity I run, hide, disappear until the danger is past. Whatever prompted me to say yes, to take the oath?

I get up, eat a piece of bread, and walk to school. The same routine as yesterday.

Ella never mentions the oath. I keep going to classes and working at the hospital, but I pester her to be involved in something secret, something important. The answer is always the same: "Wait. Your turn will come."

As all the Germans celebrate their great victory on the Russian front, one can't avoid the omnipresent "master race," parading, drinking, singing with joy and love for their führer; yet a strange counterpoint whispers through the streets of Krakow. Thousands are dying—in concentration camps, in prisons, on the streets. Most of their names are unknown, but myriad posters plastered on official buildings list hostages who have been dragged from prison cells and executed in the public square in retaliation, for a single German killed by a Pole in self-defense or in response to an atrocity. Posters bearing the names of these innocent victims of revenge are called "Poland's saddest Christmas cards."

A small pine tree decorated with bits of cotton and colored paper presides over a feast in the smoke-filled front office. Doctors and nurses from the emergency ward delivered the delicious food for this afternoon's party. Tomorrow is Christmas Eve. Friends begin to drop in to wish each other a good holiday. While recognizing faces, I remain a stranger in the midst of this noisy celebration. Even the glass of vodka gives no lift. Ella, always effervescent, is in the center, laughing without restraint, cracking another loud joke. I decide that to work with these people is a privilege, but to play with them is work. At Adampol, others were strangers and it was I who belonged.

The smell of steaming bigos, a Polish cabbage and meat dish, filters through the room. I rush to the table where the doctor has placed the huge pot and take over the serving. This delicious dish, accompanied by freshly baked bread and rolls, was always a part of the Christmas Eve hunt. Its wonderful smell, combined with the vodka, whisks me back to Adampol, where Jerome, Basia, and I dance gleefully around the festive tree.

Christmas gifts have been distributed to the servants,

who have left, and now it is time for our own. Jerome
and Basia are surrounded by boxes, large and small, but
two blackboards with the words PEARL and MERCEDES
BENZ, in white letters, are all that I can claim from under
the giant tree. Mama notices my disappointment.

"Christine, put on your coat; bundle up and run to
the stable. You will see why," she assures.

Mystified, I grab my coat and boots. Last summer
Mama asked me what I would name two horses. I run
out the door, with Tatek's voice trailing after me: "Your
own stable now, Christine."

My own stable, two stalls, a pony and a young mare,
and above the stalls, slats for the boards: PEARL and
MERCEDES BENZ! I hug them both, stroking their warm
bodies and smelling their fur. On a shelf, a saddle and
bridle, all mine.

"Please, may I have some more bigos?" asks a strange
red face, covered with perspiration.

"Of course," I answer. "I'm glad you like it, too. Here
you are."

Early the next morning Mama is in a hurry. We had
planned to search for something special for our Christmas
Eve dinner.

"But I have to be home by noon," she says firmly.

I don't pay much attention; she is always so busy that
what I do notice is how the weariness in her face
permeates her whole body, sagging her shoulders. Yet
she walks very briskly in the cold. We come upon an
unusually long line at the market.

"I'll stand in the queue, Mama. There must be something good at the other end, or there wouldn't be such a crowd. Under those potatoes and cabbages maybe there are hidden treasures. Sausage or fish, perhaps."

When I ask the people in front of me what is being sold, they confirm my suspicion: meat and fish! I wait an hour, then two. I think back on yesterday's party, how Ella's eyes sparkled with delight as she told of an old coat that her parents had given her one Christmas. The presents given to the servants' children at Adampol were far better than any she had received in her entire life, I realize. When she asked me about my favorite Christmas present, I could not tell her about Pearl and Mercedes Benz, so my dearest gift became my rabbit, Napoleon.

Nearing the end of the long line, my eyes focus on the score of baskets in front of the peasant woman, some filled with pine bouquets, some with cabbages, and others with potatoes. Young girls and boys stand on each side of her, ready to defend their goods and their lives. Should the Germans raid the marketplace, each will grab one basket and run like hell in opposite directions to protect what is tucked beneath: the fish, the meat, the forbidden things. These children know every doorway, every hiding place, I hope.

With apples in a bag tucked under one arm and good, fresh pike wrapped in an old newspaper sticking out of my coat pocket, I leave the market to look for Mama. Every penny spent, I cannot wait to show her how well I have done, but I cannot find her. I worry as I repeatedly check each corner of the market. It is ten past twelve.

Finally I spot her in front of our own gateway, talking with a stranger who seems familiar, though I cannot place him. He looks sick, eyes and cheeks sunken and hollow. As I approach him and my eyes meet his, he smiles, opens his arms toward me, and hoarsely calls my name.

"Jesus, Mary, it's Tatek," I cry. My father, my father, what have they done to him? I hug him, now so thin and so old.

"Oh, my Tatek, are you home? You will stay, never go away again?"

Tatek answers slowly. "I hope so. Apparently the Germans who took Adampol have left the area, and as they are exterminating the Jews on a mass scale, they needn't pursue me for hiding a single Jewish family. Then too, they may have caught the family. I don't know, really. I still am not sure what they knew."

"So you are safe?"

"Safe, Christine? What does that mean these days? I have been hiding four months . . . always separated . . ."

We cross the gateway and start up the stairs. Tatek stops midway and turns to us.

"This is important for you to remember. The two Gestapo who threw us out of Adampol had no legal authority to do so. If I had known that, I would have filed a complaint with their superiors and we could have remained there. The German government considered Adampol a major source of food and lumber for the Army. That was their primary reason for retaining us to help run the estate smoothly. The Gestapo wanted it for themselves and were determined to dispose of me before I filed a grievance."

Together we climb the rest of the stairs in silence. I am so glad Tatek is here but am not sure that he is forgotten by the Germans. They are like hunting dogs that never give up the trail.

At midnight, this Christmas Eve, all gather around the table set so regally in the front room. The twigs of pine placed in the center remind us of a time when green boughs filled our homes with fresh fragrance, and full bundles of wheat, barley, rye, and corn, those eternal symbols of abundance, stood witness beside our table. At Adampol, whoever pulled the longest straw from under the white linen might have the longest life. Here we have no straws, yet because all of us are alive and together, this Christmas seems more wondrous than any other.

My grandmother, Babcia, aging and unwell, joins us in celebration. Her thinness is accentuated by her long black dress, worn in remembrance of Dziadzio's death two years earlier, after their escape from the Russian zone. Pale, elegant, her face reflects joy as she takes a wafer, breaks it into a piece for each, and wishes us a blessed Christmas. We talk and sing carols long into the night.

On Christmas morning, we attend Mass in a cathedral overfilled with strangers, who turn to greet us, wish us well. Bound by the fight against misery, fear, and despair, we, standing here so close together, are able to express warmth and concern for one another. While I do not listen carefully to the Mass, I take Communion with the rest.

Natalia, Jerome, Andrew, and I linger in front of the church. We are tired of being somber and serious in the company of adults, while they talk incessantly of German atrocities. It is our right to be young, to laugh and be frivolous, we think. We want to have a party, to drink, eat, dance all night.

All the adults attend the beginning of our party. We must accept that, until their bedtime, they will sit and nod and be in the way.

One of the guests triumphantly uncorks a bottle.

"Good French wine, stolen from the Nazis."

Glasses fill, one after the other. Hands reach, old hands, young hands. Thank God there is more than one bottle! I notice Tatek and Uncle Stefan appear light and happy; but Mama has retired to her room.

Andrew winds up the gramophone. On our crowded living room dance floor we perform the slowest Viennese waltz imaginable. With the lights turned out, it does not matter if we are close in each other's arms. While I dance with Andrew, who is tipsy and hangs on to me and steps on my toes, I watch a silver sliver from the streetlight catch tall broad shoulders. I will work my way toward him, I decide. The waltz ends, the lights go on, and a voice shouts, "Next, a tango."

Not knowing how to dance a tango, I shout "*No*," snatch one of the bottles, and saunter in his direction.

"Let me pour some wine for you," I offer. "It seems you are neglected."

He puts his arm around me.

"As you can see, my glass is full. I am by no means neglected. My name is Alik. May I have the next dance?"

"Not this next one; it is spoken for. But it will be a pleasure, the one after."

I turn away.

"Christine, pour me some wine," says my brother.

"Jerome, you are a miracle!" I grab his hand and drag him to the dance floor.

"Dance with you? You move like a cow."

"Jerome, I beg you to save my life."

When I clutch his arm and whisper what I have done, he laughs jokingly. "You! Play hard to get! Well, it's not a bad method, but don't exaggerate. Next time dance with him, and be careful. You are ruining my shoes!"

Never in my life have I been in the arms of a man who kissed me while we danced, whispering all the things I wanted to hear. The rest of the evening is with Alik.

We notice how daylight takes over from the streetlamp. The record player stops, but the change in me does not.

I have argued with Mama continually since the party. I should be treated as an independent adult now that I have joined the Resistance. Mama does not agree. She does not trust me, especially with Alik, and I detest her questions about where I am going, with whom. I lie, as it is so much easier.

DISCIPLINE

The eager docility of the wartime civilian mind was never better exemplified than by an incident that took place in one of Gimbels' elevators during the gift-exchanging rush. The operator, a little minx plainly new to the job, took on a load of passengers at the ground floor, closed the door and said, in tones of authority, "Face the rear, please." Without a moment's hesitation—and certainly without a moment's thought—all the passengers faced the rear. It was such an odd sight that the operator exclaimed, "My God, that can't be right! Face the front, please!" The passengers executed another about-face. Theirs not to reason why.

The New Yorker, *January 9, 1943*

WINTER 1943

No one can live like this forever. Since 1939 the German Program has forbidden theater performances, concerts, all opportunities for social entertainment. Movie houses are open to the Polish people, but because the revenues are collected by the German Army Entertainment Committee, none of us go. *"Tylko swinie siedza w kinie"* (Only pigs sit in movies), we say.

To escape the endless dreary time, people resort to primitive pleasures. They play cards, drink, and flirt. In loneliness and uncertainty, husbands and wives separated by the war turn to other mates. Conversations may start with discussions of the German atrocities. But the early curfew, which forces friends to stay together until dawn, naturally leads to infatuation and sexual pleasure.

"It is inexpensive, not forbidden by the Germans, pleasant, and available," Ella says. And I agree.

Unlike Mama, I see nothing wrong with a man and woman finding solace in a temporary relationship if it helps them both, hurts no one, and can be forgotten as circumstances change. Before the war, table manners were important, but today not only do we eat pig's food but we eat like pigs. Why should it matter with whom we sleep?

Now that I have begun my official nurse's training, I feel I have a right to such independent views. I passed my regular high school midterm exams, all due to Ella, who tutored me right through the final morning. Actually I am bored with subjects like poetry and equations; I find nurse's training far more interesting, now that I have discovered a consolation for pain. No matter how a patient suffers, how desperate his wounds, it could be worse; I could be in his place!

The emergency room usually goes well, for Ella helps

me in tight spots and Dr. Mazur is very patient with me. But today there is a palpable tension.

"Christine, you are to go to this address." Dr. Mazur hands me a slip of paper.

"Who is Maria, and where is this street?"

"Maria's home is at least a half-hour ride on the streetcar." How I hate streetcars, always overcrowded, with so much waiting.

"Yes, Doctor, I know the general area. But how shall I find Maria there?"

"She lives on the first floor. There is a card on her door, Maria G. She expects you."

Taking a small package of medication from his desk drawer, he tells me, "You will need this for a wounded flier. He is critically ill, delirious at times from a high fever and in severe pain. He was probably shot down flying over Germany near the Polish border. He must have walked for days, perhaps weeks; with luck on his side, he wasn't captured but was found lying semiconscious on a bench in the emergency room of a small-town hospital not far from Krakow. He was dressed in civilian clothes, but soon he groaned in English, a language the hospital did not understand.

"A doctor, a member of the underground, placed him in a private room and contacted me, and we were able to move him to Maria's apartment. When I saw him, two days ago, his condition was not good. He has a broken arm and shoulder, fractured ribs, a high temperature, pneumonia, and feet covered with infected wounds from frostbite. Now, I want you to visit him as often as necessary and report to me on his condition. I hope we can save him.

"This package contains necessary medication," he continued. "Instruct Maria how to care for him when you are not there. When he is not delirious, try to get as much information as possible."

Assuring him that I will do my best, I ask about Maria.

"Well, she is not a member of the Resistance, but she is very helpful. Her husband was taken hostage, tortured, and killed. She has three children, twin boys age seven, and a two-year-old girl.

"Now you must go. The young man will need a great deal of care."

"Helping to destroy the Germans is the only pleasure I now have. They are animals, and I will do what I can to help to kill every one of them," Maria announced several hours after we met. Her harsh voice, face contorted with hatred, contrasted sharply with the demure appearance of the pleasant young blond-haired woman who had let me into her cluttered two-room apartment.

Later she told me about a Warsaw family who had a radio hidden in their bedroom. Each night the first chords of Beethoven's Fifth announced the beginning of the BBC broadcast. One afternoon on a streetcar filled with Germans the little boy began to sing those very chords. Both parents were arrested.

Maria wants to help the young flier, yet has asked to have him removed as soon as his health permits, for with three small children who could unwittingly reveal his presence at any time, there is danger for all.

The wounded man rests on a mattress placed on an oak table shoved against a corner wall in the room that is kitchen, dining room, and living room. A cupboard blocks the open side of the massive table. When Maria first pushed it away, I found a battered body that shocked me; yet I wanted to tend it, to somehow make it well again. His arm, badly swollen and bruised, was in obvious need of setting. His legs smelled foul; both feet and all the toes, severely frostbitten, were now covered with large pus-filled sores. I warned Maria that bandaging them too tightly could cause complications and that the greatest danger of all was gangrene, then amputation.

One side of his body was horribly bruised; it was an ordeal to wash him, for he groaned with pain at the slightest touch. The doctor's morphine did help, so I showed Maria how to give injections when I was not there. Though I cautioned her sternly, she remained complacently confident. One would think she were merely looking after her children's bruises and colds.

Back at Dr. Mazur's office, I describe what I have found and stress the need for X rays, for setting the arm with a cast. Underscoring the danger of serious infection and pneumonia, I conclude breathlessly, "And we have got to move him. Maria's children could give him away."

"Christine, you are absolutely right, but it is too dangerous to bring him to the hospital, so you are the one who will have to find a new place for him."

Devastated, I manage to make my voice sound casual

as I ask, "Any suggestions? I'm having a bit of a hard time thinking where to begin."

"The best thing would be the monastery, not far from here."

Pacing the room, Dr. Mazur mumbles, "Yes, the monastery, where we could drop in often and keep an eye on him."

"A monastery?"

"Yes, they have already provided shelter for many men, and I am sure they will take one more. Go see Father Jan. He is the abbot."

He jots a note, glances up at me.

"This is only an introduction. It is safer if you tell Father Jan of our predicament in person."

The monastery is surrounded by a brick wall so high I can barely see the roofs of the ancient buildings inside. Standing before its awesome iron gate, I pause a moment, then pull the bell rope.

"I wish to see Father Jan," I tell the young monk who appears.

"Father Jan is saying Mass. Come, make yourself comfortable in front of the fire."

For a time I watch the slow-burning blue flame casting shadows on the granite walls. There is little furniture: a long oak table with intricate carvings, some old wooden chairs, and above the arched doorway, a huge iron cross. The bare simplicity of this room calms my inner turbulence.

Mass ends and the monks emerge from the chapel, each in a dark brown robe tied at the waist with a white rope. The young monk approaches a tall, frail, older man. As they come toward me I notice a scar on the brow of the elder, who is introduced as Father Jan.

"What can I do for you, my child?"

"Dr. Mazur has sent me to you."

Father Jan reads my note, while I explain the situation. Without hesitating he responds, "Of course we can keep him here. We have several refugees here now. Polish Jews, Polish Catholics . . . an Allied soldier should make our community still more interesting. He will be safe with us. We all dress as monks; at times we ourselves are not sure who is who."

I am reassured but confused. Jews dressed as monks? At the nuns' school in Warsaw I was told that each year the Jews killed a Christian baby, drained its blood, and put that blood into their ritual bread.

"But he must be strong enough to walk before we move him," Dr. Mazur insists. "To carry him out of Maria's apartment into a car . . . it would be risky. I should set his broken arm next, not easy without an X ray. Anyway, the arm is the least of his problems. First we must know whether or not he will live."

"Certainly he will live," I answer defiantly. How dare he speak that way about my patient.

Ella is nowhere to be found. Is she ill? But she never is. . . .

"She is working with the Resistance," says Dr. Mazur, "distributing a truckload of captured ammunition to different parts of the city. Many people are involved. It won't take them long."

Ella carting ammunition, my soldier dying on that mattress, I work in a frenzy this afternoon, hoping one of them will survive.

Maria greets me, smiling. "Good news for you. He's better. The fever is still high but sometimes he opens his eyes and talks. I can't understand what he's saying."

When we pull aside the cupboard, his eyes open and a faint smile crosses his face as he tries to speak. I stop him.

"Hello. Everything will be all right. You are safe here, so don't try to talk, you need to save your strength. It's time to check the sores on your feet. They didn't like the cold. But can you tell me your name?"

In a tired voice, he answers, "Johnny."

I turn to Maria, as if to introduce them formally. "This is Johnny."

Johnny is asleep.

"Maria, give him morphine only when he is in unbearable pain. And be sure to space it no more often than every four hours."

She answers defiantly, "Well, I did exactly what you told me."

"Of course you did, but apparently it is too much."

Maria seems relieved about the monastery. Her children are especially restless this afternoon; watching them preoccupies her. One of the twins looks exactly like his father, she says.

"Don't you wish you were their age, Maria?"
"Childhood is a marvelous place to hide."

Mama is waiting at the gate when I get home after dark.

"You are late, Christine. You *must* be more careful about the curfew."

She is brusque as she opens the door to our apartment. Then her voice softens. "Ella is in your room."

Ella is huddled on my bed, her eyes red and swollen. Her whole body shakes as she cups her face in her hands and sobs, swaying hysterically back and forth.

"I can't go back. I need to stay here tonight.

"He was only fourteen, only fourteen, such a good-looking kid, with blue eyes full of adventure, and freckles all over his face. I think he loved this game, loved playing the role of underground soldier, hoping someday he might be commander. He would whisper to me even when it was perfectly safe to talk out loud. Yes, he was so excited about the plot that he lost sight of the real danger we were in."

She keeps staring, transfixed.

"The commanding officer ordered twelve of us to divide and transport some stolen ammunition. We packed it into boxes light enough to carry, then stuffed the top of each package with German propaganda magazines so that the whole thing looked like a bundle of Nazi newspapers. It was risky, for even with the false German permits we were likely to be stopped and searched.

"I had not met my partner before. Pietrek was only

fourteen. Our first three trips went without a hitch, almost too easy. The last trip, Pietrek and I entered the city safely, but as we approached Rynek [the marketplace] I suspected we were being followed. You see nothing, hear nothing, but you sense someone always behind. Turning a corner, I glanced over my shoulder and spotted a man in civilian clothes about thirty steps behind us. If he turned the corner too, I feared my suspicion would be confirmed.

"Pietrek talked and laughed as if he were carrying a large birthday present to his grandmother. I knew I must warn him so that he wouldn't be taken by surprise.

" 'Pietrek, keep calm, keep going and don't look back; behave as if there is nothing to worry about. Someone is following us.' He dropped the package, shouted 'Jesus-Maria,' and took off like a frightened deer. The man behind us sprang after him, ordering, 'Halt! Halt!' I was left on the sidewalk, paralyzed with fear, a box at my feet.

"Two uniformed Germans appeared out of nowhere and joined the chase." Ella continued in a stricken voice. "I heard Pietrek yell once. Then a shot . . . and silence. Shaken, I dashed through the open door of a church, hid in a confessional, and told the priest what had happened. He led me out the back door into an alley. Christine, he was only fourteen."

Ella has always seemed so strong, so in control of herself. I hold her until the sobbing stops and think how stupid, senseless! We, the Resistance Army, steal ammunition from the Germans to kill the Germans. For each one we kill, they kill ten Polish hostages. So it continues, the vicious circle getting larger and larger. I doubt if Pietrek even knew why he gave his life.

Ella stays on in my room, and night after night we replay the horror of Pietrek's death. Though we whisper, Mama senses that something shocking has happened. Very late one night, she comes to my room, sits on my bed with her hands on my shoulders, and in a tone more tender than I have ever heard from her murmurs, "It was very bad, I am sure."

Ella simply shakes her head and repeats, "Very bad."

His smile is now stronger.

"Hello, Johnny."

"Hello. You are my nurse and you haven't been here for days," he says reproachfully. "How long have I been here?"

"In this house, several weeks, but we have no idea how long you have been in Poland. Where is your home?"

"New Zealand."

Though I try to be very careful, placing two pillows as supports for his back, he moans with pain as I help him sit up. His ribs are still deep purple and black, the edges turning yellow. The sores on his feet are washed, covered with fresh dressings; a sling is made for his newly casted arm; then, with Maria's help, we bathe him.

I visit Johnny as often as I can. The only thought that

spoils my happiness is: It won't last. Don't get involved. It will hurt and it will end. Still, Mama has noticed that I answer her less sharply. The Germans, my parents, the church seem less important than the moment.

Ella returned to her own apartment after three weeks. Now, coming home from work together, we are caught in a street dragnet with almost two hundred others. Because Pietrek's death proves that running from the Germans is as dangerous as being inside the circle, we stand motionless. Twenty soldiers, guns pointed, order us all against the wall, and we all move obediently, body pressed against body, hearing one another's heartbeats, feeling our trembling fingertips touching.

I notice the black band and dreaded silver skull on the cap of the soldier beside us in the front line. He is from the S.S., the worst butchers of all. He stands, legs spread, pointing his rifle first at Ella, then me. At his feet a German shepherd growls, impatient for a command. These dogs are more feared than their masters, for they maim and mutilate before they kill.

There are shouts and screams as men, women, and children flee the apartment house across the street and are shoved viciously against the wall. The S.S. soldiers surround the group with a ring so tight not even a mouse could slip out.

"Ella," I whisper, "what is it?"

"I don't know. They caught the people in the apartment house for something."

Sensing someone looking at me, I raise my eyes and

meet those of the S.S. storm trooper. He wants me to
show the secrets hidden in my heart. He smiles at me.
Frightened, I manage to force an awkward smile.

A woman holding a baby breaks through the German
line across the street and runs toward the S.S. trooper
standing next to us. She is down on her knees in front
of him, begging.

"*Gnädiger Herr* . . . please save my baby, please, you
can kill me but not her. You see these two nurses here,
they will take my little Salecia. Please, I beg you."

The S.S. trooper looks away from the woman and at
our nurse's uniforms. He smiles again, that sinister
inviting smile, as if to say, sure, you can take the child
and save it. As I move a step forward, Ella's fingernails
dig into my arm.

"You fool," she whispers in Polish. "Don't you see
what he is doing?"

I stand rooted to the ground.

The woman still holds out her child to us, murmuring
in Yiddish. The face of the S.S. trooper twists in such a
contortion of hate that he appears demented. He holds
a braided wire riding whip. His eyes challenge mine, for
only a moment, then he turns to the kneeling woman,
picks up her baby, throws its blanket back at her, and
taking the baby by its feet, smashes its head against the
curb.

"*Verdammte Juden.*" (Damned Jews.)

The sound of the splitting skull echoes in the street
and blood splashes everywhere. There is no breathing,
no sound, and then the most piercing wail of the baby's
mother, sobbing, gasping, the blood from her child

running all over her as she tries to cradle it next to her heart.

The Germans bark a command to those of us on this side of the street.

"*Raus.*" (Get going.)

We turn and flee, all of us running blindly, not knowing where. Several blocks away, Ella and I stop in a doorway to catch our breath. There is a shot. The mother has joined her child in death.

I am learning to hate. Today I want vengeance. I will devote all of my energy toward German destruction. Happiness is to be found in their dying. It seems years ago that I had a conversation with the young German soldier at Adampol. How young and foolish I was then.

SPRING 1943

The warm April sun has never seemed more beautiful or been more welcome. Today Johnny is moving from Maria's house to the monastery. My New Zealander is truly handsome, now that his bruises have paled and his arm is free of a cast. I will be alone with him for the first time.

I wonder how often I will see Maria after this morning's transfer. She always refers to my family as "your class," for she detests the aristocracy and maintains a list of historic facts about aristocrats who were traitors and scoundrels, a list stretching back to the Middle Ages. One day I asked her why she liked me.

"It's simple. If all the aristocratic conceit and pomposity

in you has been destroyed by the war, you are no longer a part of *that* group."

Maria and Johnny are waiting. She has given Johnny all of her husband's clothes and many of his personal things.

"You will be the best-dressed man in Krakow," I exclaim.

"No! the best-dressed man in Poland!"

Maria laughs with embarrassed gratitude, but there is sadness in her face. A silence falls between the three of us. Johnny breaks it.

"Well, what do you think? Am I well dressed enough to become a monk?"

He looks very Polish with his haircut and Polish clothes. Only his accent betrays him.

"Let's walk through the park. There is more sunshine there than in the monastery," I suggest.

"Why not?" he responds, taking my hand.

Later he leads us to a park bench.

"I need a rest."

From his pocket he takes out a small box tied with red ribbon.

"It's not much, but it represents a lot. Someday I will buy you the most beautiful diamond ring you can imagine. For now, this is the best I can do . . . with one exception."

I feel shy as Johnny kisses me deeply, with great force. After a bit, I fumble with the red-ribboned box and open it. There is a silver ring with R.A.F. engraved on it. My first impulse is to put it on; then I realize the ring would betray us if we were caught by the Germans.

Father Jan greets us in the main hall of the monastery. He excuses himself and leads Johnny into the darkness while I wait.

Soon two monks appear at the far end of the hall. One is Father Jan. The other—my God, it's Johnny. The man who has just ardently kissed me on a park bench is now a monk.

No sooner do I arrive at the hospital than Dr. Mazur confronts me.

"Excellent timing, Christine. We have three more soldiers who need to be cared for. You must move them, as they are now with a family of three in a one-room apartment. The Health Clinic hospital will be willing to take them for the moment. Ask for Dr. Gajda."

"How do we know they aren't spies, Nazis playing tricks on us?"

"When you see them you will be reassured."

I am rushing out the door when he adds, "Be careful, but move them as soon as possible."

"It can't be today. I must take my math exam. . . ."

Weariness overcomes me as I settle on the streetcar banquette riding home after the exam. Today was exhausting. Some days I must travel to as many as four different homes for classes now that the nuns' school is closed. The Germans stormed the convent in March, then tortured and killed one of the nuns after some younger students had been arrested, beaten, and "confessed" to the real nature of the school.

The streetcar stops with a terrible jerk.

"Alles raus, alles raus!" (Everyone out!)

Police shove us onto the sidewalk. A colonel orders us to present our I.D. cards. He examines each one closely. I pass him mine. He hesitates, looks at both sides, passes it to a corporal who is collecting them, and moves on.

Uncle Stefan stands across the street watching. Impulsively, I wave my arms and *know* he sees me. Without the slightest sign of recognition, he turns and moves away. A German soldier asks me who I am waving at. "How stupid of me," I answer. "I thought I saw my mother."

"Then perhaps, *Fräulein*, you would like her to join you."

He looks, but there are only shadows moving into the distance.

For two hours the Germans herd more and more people into the ring. The old, the crippled, and small children are released immediately. The young will be sent to labor camps in Germany. At least Uncle Stefan saw me, so Mama and Tatek will know I have not been executed. Execution might be preferable; the labor camps are a slower death.

When my name is called, I duck, trying to hide, only to hear it called again. There is no escape. An officer who is standing with a grossly overfed civilian hands me my I.D. card.

"Gehen sie." (Go.)

The civilian takes my arm, muttering *"Schnell, schnell."* (Hurry, hurry.) At the end of a back alley I collapse into Uncle Stefan's arms. He addresses the little fat man as

Herr Weisenbek, shakes his hand, then grabs my arm, suggesting that we move quickly.

"When I saw you in the group of prisoners I rushed to Herr Weisenbek, a prewar Austrian friend, who is now director of a transportation company affiliated with the German Army. He employs several Polish people, so when he heard what had happened he immediately came out to reclaim you as one of his employees."

"But my I.D. says that I work at the hospital."

"He knew that. Obviously your hospital employment card doesn't mean a damn to the Germans. Tomorrow, Weisenbek will provide you with a new, fictitious I.D., and officially you will be working for him. You will be much safer, and it should be a great help in your work with the Resistance."

"You *know*?" I utter, dumfounded.

"My dear Christine. I am not as dumb as you think."

"You need not do any work here, yet you should appear a few times each week."

Sitting opposite me, Herr Weisenbek looks like a Notre Dame gargoyle, but a friendly one. After my warm thank you, he begins to reminisce about his boyhood friendship with Uncle Stefan, their school years in Vienna.

"I am very fond of him, Christine, and was glad I could be of some help yesterday. If you are ever in trouble again, do not hesitate to ask my assistance. I will do all that I can."

■ ■ ■

Visiting Herr Weisenbek's office these past two weeks, I got to know another Polish girl who "works" there. Weisenbek often turns on the radio, then leaves the room, allowing us time to tune in an English station for news from the Allied front and to sample food from the ever-available gourmet snack trays. When he returns, he is smiling. Perhaps he is torn by his current situation and we are his means of balancing it.

Dr. Mazur has taken thorough advantage of Herr Weisenbek's kindness.

"Ask him for a curfew pass. The Resistance desperately needs one and we have printers who can make exact copies."

With my most innocent smile, I ask Weisenbek for the pass.

"*Mein liebes Fräulein,* I have no such authority. I know how difficult it must be for you to travel from home to the hospital within curfew hours. Perhaps . . . yes! My Austrian friend, Herr Schrek, might be able to make the arrangements for you. I will request an appointment."

That same afternoon I take the streetcar to Herr Schrek's office. When I finally obtain a seat in the rear (only Germans are allowed to ride in front), a tottering man, reeking of vodka, plops down beside me. Standing without warning, he grabs the bar above his head and bellows at the Germans in the forward section of the car. Nothing will quiet him.

"That son of a bitch, that fuckin' bastard. I hope he rots in hell, the fucking murderer."

A civilian, the hated *Hakenkreuz* pinned to his lapel, jumps the dividing rope and grabs the drunk by the neck.

"You are under arrest."

"And for what are you arresting me, Mr. Gestapo? I have done nothing wrong."

The German tightens his grip around the man's throat.

"And whom were you cursing, swine?"

The drunk's eyes open wide in amazement at the question.

"Churchill, of course. Whom did you think I was cursing, Mr. Gestapo?"

Confused and embarrassed, the German retreats while the drunk looks straight ahead, his eyes fixed like steel on the Germans in the front of the car. I am roaring with laughter inside, but I do not even smile.

Herr Schrek greets me in his waiting room.

"Ah yes, you are the young nurse who needs a curfew pass. Today I am terribly busy. Before I can speak with you, I must finish. . . ."

Alone again in the waiting room, I fumble for a cigarette. I remove an underground newspaper from my stuffed pocket, finding a cigarette beneath. Just as I light it, Herr Schrek calls for me.

"Now tell me again, precisely what is it that you need?"

I tell him and carefully list the reasons I think will be most convincing.

"*Liebes Fräulein.* I am very sorry, but that I cannot issue you." I stare at the pile of blank curfew passes spread on the desk between us.

"It is much easier for the hospital to rearrange your hours than it is for me to issue a curfew pass!"

His voice drones on. Feigning shyness, I lower my eyes to the desk.

"My goodness, I have talked so much my mouth is dry. Might I ask for a glass of water?"

"Of course, *Fräulein*. Let me pour it for you."

As Herr Schrek hands me the glass of water, I clumsily let it drop on the silver tray. Other glasses fall to the floor; water soaks the desk and rug.

"Oh, Herr Schrek, I am so embarrassed, so sorry. I will clean it up."

Allowing no protest, on my hands and knees I start gathering bits of glass from the rug beneath the desk. Herr Schrek, as a good Austrian gentleman, kneels down to help. With a fist full of broken glass in my right hand I jump up, throw it noisily on the tray while slipping a curfew pass into my blouse, then stoop back to the floor to resume the cleaning.

"Don't worry about the glasses. I hope you have no difficulty in changing your hours," Herr Schrek cordially concludes.

When I next enter Herr Weisenbek's office, the radio isn't on. He does not smile.

"*Fräulein*, you are to go to Herr Schrek's office immediately. He expects you. Go, *now!*"

Herr Schrek greets me with the same courtesy.

"I asked you to come because I think you lost something the last time you were here."

He hands me a paper from his desk drawer, the Polish underground newspaper from my pocket.

"I—I have never seen it before," I manage to stammer.

"Fräulein, Sie haben mehr Glück als Verstand." (Young lady, you have more luck than brains.)

He strikes a match and burns the paper over a wastebasket.

"Now, go. Be careful, for the games you play are not for children. Losses are counted in human lives."

A few days ago I stole from this man, despised him as the enemy because he was German and would have celebrated his death. Now, because of him, I walk out free. I feel uncomfortable, unclean. Herr Schrek's human act has made me a debtor to a German. I am so ashamed.

=== MEASURES OF ===
IMMEDIATE AID

The Jews receive practically none of the essential protective and vitamin foods. They get no meat, fish, poultry, milk, dairy products, fruit or vegetables. They may purchase none of the goods which are still unrationed, none of the items which are distributed on the basis of the consumer lists, none of the semi-rationed items. More and more rationed staples are entirely denied to them; and of such rationed food as they may still receive, they are allotted not more than half of the normal rations. As a rule, the weekly rations for Jews in Polish ghettos amount at best to a pound of black bread, two ounces of so-called jams or marmalade, one ounce of sugar, and perhaps a few potatoes. They receive no other food. Four hundred calories is the daily ration of a ghetto-Jew as compared with the nutritional minimum of 3,000.

The New Republic, *August 30, 1943*

SUMMER 1943

The first sound is water, pushed by a gentle wind against the shore of the lake. Johnny's arms around me, I lazily remember last night. It was the first time. I roll over and stretch to feel the morning sunlight.

"Christine, will you marry me? When this goddamn holocaust is over, will you marry me?"

I am startled.

"How do you know we will survive it?"

"I don't, but if . . . will you?"

Hesitating, unable to answer, my mind is clogged with questions about Johnny. For weeks he has been dressed like a monk, always chaperoned, and each time I saw him it was like taking tea with an old-maid aunt. How can I be sure what I feel about him? Occasionally Ella and I would arrange a party for the English and New Zealand soldiers at her apartment. The phonograph records were old and raspy, the girls were vulgar, and the vodka stank. When he caressed me too much in front of the others, I was uncomfortable. His behavior displeased me, particularly his flirtations with other girls. Will he love only me?

His eyes light up when he talks about his home in New Zealand. He wants me to go there, but would I leave Poland? I need time to decide.

A month ago, Aunt Renia came to the house in Krakow. One of the lucky ones, she still has her estate, only a three-hour train ride from the city. She invited me to visit her and bring Ella and Johnny.

For almost a week we have enjoyed my cousins, the lovely house, and freedom from the constant presence of Germans. Aunt Renia's lunch table holds more fresh food than the three of us have scavenged in months. We can laugh without being afraid.

In the afternoon we saddled the horses and rode more than an hour, chasing each other, to the top of a rocky hill, where we saw the lake in the distance.

After we returned to the house Aunt Renia suggested, "It is a long way to the lake; you may not be able to return before dark, and that is dangerous, especially for you, John. Germans patrol that road. Better camp by the lake and return in the morning. I will prepare a basket of food."

"Christine, marry me. It is something to live for!" Johnny's voice is impatient.

"Yes, Johnny, I will marry you. I love you. But *les rêves qui restent rêves sont toujours les plus beaux.*" (The dreams that remain dreams are always the most beautiful.)

We lie together a long time. Already I wonder about my promise.

Walking home, I tell him I think he should stay in the country for a while.

"The rest and sunshine will do you good. I can see so little of you in the monastery . . . in your long brown robe. Besides, I could never make love with a priest."

"Tell me what happened," Ella implores.

"Oh, Ella, don't be foolish. Nothing happened."

"Yes it did!"

Thank God Aunt Renia calls us.

"You mustn't miss the afternoon train to Krakow. It will be very crowded."

Johnny openly kisses me goodbye. It makes me a bit uneasy, but I want my cousins to see it. They do!

As the train emerges from the station, an old peasant woman leans forward. "Ladies, could you do me a favor? I am bringing back some food from the country, I have too many parcels. If the Germans search and find it all belongs to me, they will confiscate it and perhaps arrest me. It would be a great help if you would say that the box on the rack is yours. Would you?"

The Germans seldom allow a train into the city without inspection, and today is no exception. The old peasant pretends to be rummaging through her bag. Ella concentrates on a newspaper while I gaze out the window.

"Is that all you have?" the German inspector asks, looking at my single bag.

"Yes, that is all."

Ella kicks my leg and mumbles in Polish, "Don't forget the package the woman asked you to smuggle for her."

"Oh, yes," I say in German, "I forgot I have one box up there on the rack."

"What is it?"

"Eggs, from my aunt's farm."

"Is that actually your box?"

Although it seems like a strange question, I answer, "Yes!"

"All right, take it down and open it!"

The box is so heavy that I can barely lift it.

"If those are eggs, then I am the King of Spain," I whisper to Ella, whose voice icily pronounces, "She is gone, left the moment you stood up."

As we start to untie the string, the German touches my arm, saying, "Are you telling the truth? Is that your box?"

"Yes. Why do you ask so many times?"

The opened box is full of ammunition. I look at Ella, she at me, as the blood drains from our faces. We are caught by our own stupidity.

"Christine, it is the end."

It seems as if the whole compartment has stopped breathing; we are hunted animals waiting for the shot to be fired.

"You should not lie," the German says in perfect Polish. "You are lucky that I understood everything you said. I too am Polish, from Silesia, and not German. Do you know what would have happened if one of the others had been here?" He does not wait for an answer as he closes the box, ties the string, picks it up, walks out, and latches the door.

A group of people on the platform is surrounded by soldiers, and I try to see if the old peasant woman is there. The train is moving too fast to tell. Krakow is just ten minutes away.

THE RESPONSIBILITY OF THE DEMOCRACIES

"From the latest information it is evident that the Germans with ruthless cruelty are now murdering the few remaining Jews in Poland. Behind the walls of the ghettos the last act of a tragedy unprecedented in history is being performed. The responsibility for this crime falls in the first instance on the perpetrators, but indirectly it weighs on the whole of humanity, the peoples and governments of the Allied States, which so far have made no effort toward concrete action for the purpose of curtailing this crime."

These words are extracted from a letter written to the late Prime Minister of Poland, General Sikorski, in May of this year by Samuel Zygielbojm, one of the representatives of the Jewish population in the Polish National Council. Receiving day by day as he did authentic information of the most appalling character from underground sources, he had sought for many months in vain to move Allied statesmen in London to vigorous action. . . .

He was driven to the desperate expedient of suicide in an effort to awaken the conscience of the world, and this letter was found among his effects in his London flat. "By my death," he wrote, "I wish to express my strongest protest against the inactivity with which the world is looking on and permitting the extermination of the Jewish people."

The New Republic, *August 30, 1943*

FALL 1943

It is already November. I open our apartment door and again ask Mama, "Is there any word?"

Mama shakes her head.

"Perhaps tomorrow, Christine."

That is what she says every day. I watch her stir the soup, a brown rotten liquid, and wonder how she can continue. For two months, nothing has changed. So many gone!

The end of August was beautiful. Twice I went back to Aunt Renia's to see Johnny, where life was happy— a vacation from reality.

The third of September someone informed the Germans that Uncle Durakowski was Jewish. He fled to

Warsaw pretending to be a Hungarian army officer, was arrested and sent to Auschwitz. Uncle Stefan denied any knowledge of a Jew living in his house when the Germans came to question. Apparently the Gestapo did not believe him, for two weeks later he was taken away.

One day as I was returning home for lunch I was startled to see a small group of people gathered in front of our house. They were staring across the street at a police lorry. To my horror, in the lorry was Aunt Krystyna. As I stood rooted to the ground, out of our gateway came Tatek, Uncle Stefan, and an escort of German police with revolvers drawn. They all crossed the street, mounted the truck, and drove away before I could catch my breath.

I rushed upstairs and into the dining room. There were Uncle Stefan's and Aunt Krystyna's two boys, sobbing, Natalia trying to quiet them down, and their nanny slumped in a chair, moaning.

"Mama, what happened?" I cried.

"Christine, I am afraid it is *us* now. So terrible!"

She told me how this morning at dawn the Gestapo raided the apartment of Mr. and Mrs. Majko. Somebody had informed them that a general of the Resistance was spending the night there. They did not find him, so they took Mr. and Mrs. Majko. As Aunt Krystyna was coming back from her shopping, she was told about it by people who were standing there, and the first thing she asked was "What about the children?" "I suppose," someone volunteered, "they must still be there." We all knew there were twin girls about five or six years old. Aunt Krystyna, saying "Poor kids, all alone," went straight into the house and took the elevator to the second floor. The doorman of the house rushed after her to stop her, but was too late. He heard the door of the Majkos' apartment slam shut, so he came quickly over here to warn Uncle Stefan.

"Then the doorbell rang and four Gestapo men came in with drawn handguns," Mama said. "They frisked Tatek and Stefan and ordered them to sit down; they made the rest of us, the boys and me, sit around the card table. The children were terribly frightened, so I kept talking to them very quietly; I was afraid the Germans would hit them, and that would have been too much for your father and your uncle. One of those Nazis was in civilian clothes, a despicable-looking creature. He got up and, waving his gun at me, ordered me to go in front of him to inspect every room in the apartment. As we were passing the front door, the bell rang. I opened the door and there stood the little girl who comes to play with the boys. I stooped as though to kiss her, and managed to whisper, 'Tell Andrew to run away.' Off she went like a streak of lightning, and I was prodded with that gun into the next room. He thought he would be faced with bullets, so he kept me in front of him.

"When we entered the kitchen, I heard the back stair door slam with a bang, and he heard it too. He pushed me aside and ran, but you know how that latch slips and locks the door—you can't open it without a key. He tried with a whole series of *verflucht*s and *verdammt*s, but he did not look for the key, and it was lying right there on the floor, only I had my foot on it. Then he made me go back to the dining room, where two more Germans had come. They took Tatek and Uncle Stefan and we saw them and Aunt Krystyna driven away.''

I went to my room and burst into tears. Now it was my father, whom I loved so much. He was gone, perhaps never to return. As I looked at a picture of Christ that was hanging above my bed I cried out loud, "Where are You, and what the hell are You doing? If You are so good, and almighty, why don't you stop the goddamn Nazis?"

I did not sleep that night at all, and in the early morning I went to Mama's room, sat on her bed, and asked her, "If it is true that God is all good, all just, and almighty, why did He allow this to happen?"

Mother looked at me, and putting her arm on my shoulder, answered, "I think that we cannot blame God for what the people do. The Lord uses those happenings for His own plans. The only thing to do is to ask for His help, which if you ask hard enough, He always sends in some unostentatious manner which we call coincidence. It is up to us how to use those coincidences. And we must always remember that this life is just a part of our existence, a sort of episode, a trial."

I looked at my mother with great admiration. She was able to accept the worst tragedy with calm that only faith can give. Her answer to my question was so simple, yet it was far beyond my comprehension. It was not only a tragedy for me but also for Andrew, Jerome, and Basia. We spent many evenings talking and trying to find a way to help to save our loved ones.

■ ■ ■

By the middle of October, Mama was frail from exhaustion and was finally confined to bed with a severe case of flu. Andrew was sent for her medicine and returned with it and a bottle of expensive French wine, which we assumed he had pinched for her.

"I didn't steal it. I was standing in line at the pharmacy and I met this man, Mr. Anthony . . . a friend of my father."

Andrew was proven blameless. Mama didn't know Mr. Anthony but several days later went with Andrew to personally thank him for the wine. Not only was he a loyal friend of Andrew's father, the murdered papal chamberlain, but he had many significant connections, including a good lawyer, Mr. Nolau. He was our last hope.

Tatek and Stefan are on the execution list, a chimney sweep who works at the prison informed Mama this morning. The Polish prison employees are almost a network; they bring information and smuggle notes to prisoners from their families.

Now at Mr. Nolau's office with Aunt Erika to translate, Mama pleads with the lawyer. Unmoved, he asks, "How much can you pay?"

"We have nothing. All of our possessions were confiscated with the estate."

Nolau's eyes brighten.

"Countess, with your name, you must have had a significant collection of jewelry."

"Yes, I had beautiful jewels. The Gestapo took them all."

"They had no right to do that!" he retorts angrily.

"Who speaks of rights these days?" Mama replies.

"We Germans have laws that must be followed. Do you remember the name of the Gestapo officer who confiscated your home?"

Mama, who rarely remembers names, does in this case. Nolau stiffens, his face turning crafty and cruel.

"If I succeed in obtaining the release of your three relatives and restore your jewels, will you give me one half of them?"

Mama agrees. Nolau says she will hear from him within ten days.

DECEMBER 1943

The chimney sweep brings his weekly report from the prison: Tatek and Uncle Stefan have not been executed. But we still have no word from Nolau.

Germans are no longer safe in Poland. As they lose the war, their increasing atrocities have galvanized the entire country into resistance. Trains are blown up, warehouses with German provisions are robbed and burned. Doctors daily risk their lives declaring people ill when they are not. The monasteries swarm with artificial monks, and Father Jan tells me that one of the convents has twenty more fake nuns than real ones.

Although every member of my family participates in this rebellion, it is Uncle Stefan's sister, Aunt Rose Potocka, who has become our heroine. Her life has been so tragic that it has made her not quite normal. Her daughter died at only nine and her son at fifteen. Uncle Thomas, her husband, is in a prisoner of war camp. She lives in a single attic room of her house with her collection of stray dogs and cats while the Gestapo occupy the rest. They keep her there, tolerating her animals along with other peculiarities, because they need her to translate Polish into German for them.

When she discovered that most arrests originated in the Gestapo headquarters of her home, Aunt Rose plugged up the downstairs toilet, then asked a plumber to come fix it. The "plumber," who fixed the toilet, installed a telephone extension from the Gestapo office to her attic room. Each time she hears anything significant, she takes one of her dogs for a walk and informs the Resistance. Aunt Rose wishes no German safe in Poland.

Advent: preparation for Christmas. A time of joy and hope and peace.

Basia and I sit with Mama in Tatek's room trying to repair his bedspread. I doubt that he will ever return to use it, but say nothing, as I don't want to dash Mama's belief in her prayers for his safe return. A flock of pigeons watches us from the balcony.

"I must feed them," she murmurs, throwing open the window to scatter some crumbs. "There, they will feel better. We are also hungry but can manage better than they."

It is so typical of Mama; somehow *we* must always manage.

Then a knock at the front door, and another.

"I wish to speak either with Countess Zamoyska or Prince Lubomirski."

Although confused by this German soldier, who has acknowledged our titles while making his request in Polish, Mama replies, "I am Zamoyska."

He furtively glances about, then lowers his voice. "I come from Auschwitz, where I am stationed and where I saw my Uncle Scharff before he died of spotted fever. He told me of your kindnesses and asked me to find you, to express his gratitude to each of you."

I recall watching Uncle Durakowski-Scharff at the gate. Now he is dead. Sorrow is followed by relief. Thank God it wasn't Tatek.

Another week passes with no word from Nolau. Ella and I are again hiding Allied soldiers. One, an American named David, young and full of energy, could never be cooped up in a monastery, so we find him shelter on a chicken farm, the perfect place. There he can roam about, help with chores, and torment the farmer's two daughters.

The second soldier is English, twenty years old but he looks sixteen. One of our hospital doctors claims him as his deaf-mute son. This identity will help him survive in case of arrest.

Two others take refuge with a lumberman, a Resistance member who lives deep in the Karpaty Forest. The Germans, fearing for their lives, are unlikely to search such remote areas.

Hearing unfamiliar shuffling feet on the stairs, our eyes all look toward Mama. The door is locked but she is unwilling to approach it. When the creaking handle turns, she demands, "Who are you, and what do you want?"

The answer, barely audible: "Stefan and I."

We find two broken shadows, with bones showing, hollow eyes. Their·clothes hang like curtains rotted by age and wind. Tatek's are covered with blood.

"Krystyna?" Mama's eyes search behind them but Tatek and Uncle Stefan shake their heads.

It is necessary to put Tatek in a tub of warm water to soak off his clothes so as not to reopen the wounds on his back. Severely beaten, physically and mentally exhausted, both he and Uncle Stefan barely speak for three days.

I decide to ask Dr. Mazur's advice as to their care. He most kindly offers an array of medicines.

I return home to find Natalia washing poor Aunt Krystyna's forehead. Aunt Krystyna just stares blankly ahead.

"How did she get here? What have they done to her? Will she live?"

Mama answers wearily. "They released her from the prison this morning. Apparently she stumbled home, barely able to find her way. No one knew until she appeared at the door. Eventually she may be all right."

It seems this room contains three ghosts, one sitting and two standing. They are fifty years older than three months ago: Tatek's black hair solid gray, Uncle Stefan's erect youthfulness bent, and Aunt Krystyna a hollow-eyed skeleton who cannot speak.

I retreat to my room.

"Damn You, *damn You*, because You probably don't exist." I have had enough of God!

Mama saw Nolau today. The jewels were heaped in a pile on his desk. She was astonished that they were all there, that the Gestapo hadn't sold them long ago.

Nolau methodically separated the jewels into two even piles, then scooped Mama's pile into a bag, saying, "There you are, Mrs. Zamoyska, and as agreed the rest are mine. Thank you, and good day."

Reflectively, Mama tells us, "You see, this whole thing shows what the true values are in life. For generations those jewels were passed from father to son and treasured as the most precious family heirlooms. Today I gave them up as if they were just gravel."

Then one day something happened which gave courage to everyone. It concerned Prince Adam Stefan Sapieha, Archbishop of Krakow, who was our relative. He was one of the most respected and loved persons in Poland, a man of proverbial integrity and courage—a bishop to his people. His unbending attitude and his terse replies to the Germans were constantly quoted. He represented all that was brave and noble.

The German governor-general of Poland was named Hans Frank. He had tried to get the archbishop to pay him a visit at Wawel Castle, the old residence of Polish kings, which he occupied as his headquarters. It would have been very advantageous for the Germans to be able to boast that the archbishop had acknowledged their supremacy.

But our archbishop was not to be pushed about. He replied that the archbishop could receive a visit but not pay one, and that throughout past centuries the kings of Poland had observed that rule.

So after a few weeks, Frank announced he would come to dinner with his staff.

Archbishop Prince Sapieha received him with the utmost politeness, but when they sat down to dinner, the menu consisted only of the food we all received on German ration cards: black bread full of bran, dark-flour noodles without butter or gravy, and beet-root marmalade, made without sugar and smelly, moldy. "Ersatz" coffee, a foul-tasting substitute, completed the meal. All of it was served on the beautiful family china, which made everything look and taste even worse.

The archbishop said he was sorry he could not give them anything better, but that was what all Poles were supposed to live on.

As the story rushes like wind through the streets of Krakow, in the cold December of 1943, the city is wild with joy. It is a new wind for the coming of a new year.

SPRING AND SUMMER 1944

Tatek, Uncle Stefan, and Aunt Krystyna have improved, but seldom speak of their experiences. They look so old.

Only eighteen, I too feel old, tired, plagued by terror. Weisenbek's I.D. card no longer protects me. The retreating Germans, preparing a futile defense of Krakow in anticipation of the Russian advance, commandeer entire city blocks to help dig trenches and plant land mines. Yesterday Ella and I were among those commandeered. A German officer registered each name, ordered us to report every day to the same location, then shoved us onto a truck to the work area. Loudspeakers blared, "If you do not return each day, your family will be sent to a labor camp in Germany."

Every detainee, given a spade and a length of ditch to dig, is told, "There is no acceptable excuse for noncompletion." No rest is allowed. Those who disobey are lashed with whips, shoved with rifle butts.

After two hours of digging my arms feel like heavy blocks of wood, the palms of my hands are raw and bleeding. A guard who looks at my hands, then Ella's, is sympathetic. Because of our nurse's uniforms he will try to place us on an ambulance truck.

Now on the truck these last hours seem easier, although we feel guilty about the others left to work in the ditches. We want to be safe, but not to be saved by a German.

After we work in the ditch a second day, the soldier who first rescued us suggests that from now on I wear my nurse's uniform, to get permanently assigned to a first-aid truck. The young Kraut has taken a liking to me.

The first-aid job, seemingly easy at first, becomes exceedingly difficult. I am to excuse the sick and injured from heavy work and give out rest permits. Within hours, more than twenty people lie near the truck, moaning dramatically each time a soldier passes by. I hate having German "authority" and am angered by those who take advantage, as they jeopardize all of us. Observing the charade, the Germans order everyone back to work. I am sent to the minefields as punishment for my "leniency."

There is an explosion not far from where we are planting mines. I ask an officer for permission to tend the wounded man.

"*Fräulein*, that man doesn't need any of your first aid," the officer says. "He is beautifully spread over the field and will make excellent fertilizer for the fall planting."

Burying mines is not physically strenuous. The mines look harmless enough, like two small plates, which we place just beneath the topsoil, but remembering the exact location of each one produces unbearable stress.

Most evenings, riding back to Krakow, the German soldier finds a seat beside me. Tonight he leans suggestively close, then whispers, "Tomorrow become sick. Do anything you can to avoid coming. The whole transport will not be digging ditches near Rzeszow. They will be shipped to Germany."

"You must leave the city," my parents say in unison when I tell them of the warning.

"*No*! I won't!"

We finally agree on an alternative plan.

Hundreds of people with additional trucks converge at the meeting point. I appear with one hand on my forehead, the other clutching my stomach, as if in excruciating pain. The transport officer reaches out to prevent my falling, then accompanies me to the entrance of a house, where I sit on the steps while he asks my name and crosses out Christine Zamoyska from the list.

"Can I call someone to take you home?"

With a shaky voice I thank him and say, "No, after a bit of rest, I think I can make it." As soon as he is out of sight, I stand up, bend way over, shuffle to the next corner, then run like hell.

Mama arranges to have me admitted to a private hospital on the far side of the city. The admission procedure complete, unforeseen torture begins. They pump my stomach, forbid me to eat, give me injections, and as all results are negative, begin another series of tests.

"Mama, I think the German camp might have been better than this."

"Christine, how can you say such things. I have good news. Uncle Stefan contacted Weisenbek. He has managed to have you classified as permanently disabled."

■ ■ ■

My father Tatek, Jerome, and my sister Basia in the woods at Adampol.

The last summer vacation; Adampol, late August 1939. We cousins getting ready to fight the Germans, and delighted by the government announcement that schools won't open September first. Front row: Marysia Tyszkiewicz, Basia, myself, Arthur Tyszkiewicz. Back row: Natalia Lubomirska, Lula Tyszkiewicz, Bisia Tyszkiewicz, Elizabeth Lubomirska, Jas Tyszkiewicz.

Rozanka, 1900. The old castle of my father's family, which was totally destroyed in World War I.

Family members and retainers bringing the miraculously spared Rozanka Madonna in a procession from Rozanka to the chapel at Adampol.

Niegoszowice, the home of Aunt Sophie Rostworowska (where she hid Jewish families during the war).

Aunt Sophie Rostworowska.

My father Tatek at the Racing Club in Warsaw, 1939.

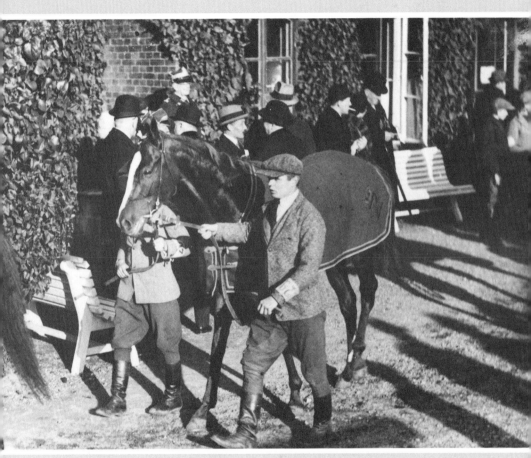

Our Warsaw Derby winner, Essor.

Wild boar trophies
displayed after a hunt at
the Dawidgródek estate
of the Radziwill family.

Wild boar shoot in the 1920s at Antoniny, the estate of Count Józef Potocki. Left to right:
Artur Sliwinski, Prince Hubert Lubomirski, Margrave Aleksandr Wielopolski, Prince
Adam Lubomirski, Count Ksawery Branicki, Count Zdzislaw Tarnowski, Count Roman
Potocki, Prince Stanislaw Lubomirski, Count Józef Potocki (the host), Count Florjan
Zamoyski, Count August Stanislaw Potocki, Prince Zdzislaw Lubomirski, Prince Pawel
Sapieha, Count Tomasz Zamoyski.

Myself, paining in Back Bay, Boston, 1960.

The train stops. I gather up my belongings, including a food package from Weisenbek containing tea, coffee, chocolate, biscuits, canned meats—the kind his office sends to Germans on the Russian front. Aunt Sophie will be delighted.

A light drizzle splatters my face on this summer day as I walk the mile through meadows and fields to her house.

Aunt Sophie is fat, wonderful, and ugly; her nose almost touches her forehead. But she is sympathetic, outgoing, warm, such a contrast to my mother, who is patrician, reserved, and cool. Aunt Sophie would hug and kiss all of us. I was her most beloved niece. Even after I was fully grown, five feet eight and a half inches tall, she would ask me to sit on her lap as if I were a baby. I loved it.

Now, at her house, it is just as I anticipated. While we devour the delicious breakfast, complete with Weisenbek's coffee, Aunt Sophie fusses over me. "We will do something about your paleness, Christine. It must have been dreadful for you."

Uncounted hours later we are still talking, when we hear a German truck roar up to the front door. A group of S.S. soldiers surrounds the house. They crash through the door and seize Sophie's sons, Andrew and Stash, whom they push out into the rain. Alisia, Sophie's daughter, cringes at the unbearably harsh voice of a soldier ordering her to walk in front of him toward the barn. His fluent Polish identifies him as a German from Silesia. He taunts, "You will never see your brothers again. All of you are a ring of thieves, robbing our transports of coal, food, and ammunition. Your house will be searched, every corner, until we find what you have hidden here."

Traveling west to east, German trains approaching the Russian front pass Aunt Sophie's farm. Polish railway workers steal supplies, then throw them from the train as it passes a forest or field. An informer has accused Aunt Sophie of being a recipient of the stolen goods.

She whispers to me, "Four Jews upstairs, guns, and hundreds of false documents."

My heart stops.

Aunt Sophie can whisper nothing more. It is traumatic enough to be accused of robbing trains, but to be caught hiding Jews . . . This vacation will end in death, I think, as I clutch my aunt, not so much to comfort her as to comfort myself. Now handcuffed, Andrew and Stash are pushed back into the house. As we stare at each other with silent knowledge that the instant the Jews are discovered all of us will be shot, one of the S.S. soldiers turns to Aunt Sophie and asks, "What is in the room upstairs?"

Responding in fluent German, Aunt Sophie, no longer the frightened old woman, smiles, leans back a little, and laughs.

"Upstairs? Ah, now why don't you go up there? You will find many Jews, guns, hundreds of false documents . . . and here are the keys."

She throws the keys on the table and motions the German toward the stairs. The Germans burst out laughing. One of them pats Aunt Sophie on the shoulder.

"Old lady, you have quite a sense of humor."

He picks up the keys, twirls them around, and hands them back to her.

"We have found nothing here. No family so filled with good humor would ever steal or be guilty of a crime against the Germans. We have searched your barn and stables, we have been through your house, and there is nothing."

Releasing the handcuffs on Andrew and Stash, one of the Germans sits down with us at the table. He speaks, we listen.

"One day we will win this war and Germany will become master of the world—"

Another interrupts him. "Your house is beautiful, its architecture. It would be a rest for me if I could come here for a vacation from hunting Jews. We will never catch all of them, even if they do pollute our civilization. . . . I would love to come here and sit in the garden."

He drones on and on. Repulsed by what he says, we smile and pretend to enjoy his conversation. Aunt Sophie, the center of attention, thanks each of them for their comments about her home. Acting more kindly now, as if nothing has happened, they offer good cigarettes to each of us. "It is unfortunate that nice people like you, who are not criminals, have to be treated the same way as guilty Polish swine."

Another German admires the shawl that Aunt Sophie has thrown over her shoulders. She offers it to him, saying, "Here, take it as a souvenir from this house. It will remind you of the good time we had together."

The German, not sensing the irony, accepts the shawl, then offers her a bag full of cigarettes.

"Thank you, but I dare not accept *your* gift. I would love the cigarettes, as they are so much better than those we are used to these days. Should another outfit like yours come here and find a bag full of cigarettes— German cigarettes, at that—they would arrest me for stealing."

The Germans roar with laughter, commenting on the old lady's wisdom. Aunt Sophie stands erect by the table while the Germans retreat to their truck.

"Quick," she whispers, "go upstairs. Tell them it is safe."

Andrew, Alisia, and I run upstairs, unlock the door, but see no one. Andrew calls out, "It is safe!"

A faint noise comes from one of the trunks, then gasping breaths. Standing, stretching, these solemn, sticklike figures have eyes that peer through a thousand years.

FALL 1944

Of all that I had heard and had lived through, now with August 1, 1944, came the worst tragedy for us Poles: the uprising of Warsaw.

The Russians were at the gates of the city, on one side of the River Vistula. They had the suburbs of the capital. On the other side of the river the Germans were arresting and killing people by the hundreds. Driven to exasperation and egged on by the Russian radio, the people rose. The brutality of the Germans was unsurpassed; many of my relatives and friends lost their lives. While men, women, and children were fighting for their lives, across the river, the Allied Russian Army was waiting for the Germans to clear the town. House by house was systematically destroyed, while people hid in sewers, died in the rubble. It was hell on earth.

Refugees from Warsaw began to arrive in Krakow. They brought more and more details about the fight. While underground soldiers were armed with revolvers, rifles, and machine guns, the Germans used planes, tanks, and heavy artillery. It was only when the uprising was completely stifled and Warsaw was utterly destroyed that the German-Russian war was resumed. The Germans, enraged at the turn of the war, sought to take out their spite on the Polish population. Life became intolerable.

And then one day, just before the surrender of Warsaw, my school friend Anusia appeared at our house in Krakow, her face bruised and pale, legs swollen, and one arm badly burnt. She was one of the last people to abandon the ruins of *State Masteo* (the Old City). The Germans were attacking all around and the tanks were almost at arm's reach. She and the others had only one way of escape: through the sewers. She realized that it was very risky, because if the Germans became aware of this, they would throw a few grenades down the manholes and massacre everybody in the tunnels. The tunnels had already been used by others, and horrible things happened to Anusia's friends. Germans caught these poor people while they were entering the sewers, stood waiting until all of them climbed down, then opened the manholes and poured down petrol and burned them alive. But for Anusia and her friends this was the only way. In knee-deep water, in excrement and in appalling stench, and carrying her newborn baby, she and her friends walked bent in half for about three miles. On and off they were able to catch a whiff of fresh air when they passed under an open manhole. When they finally emerged from the tunnel, they were captured by the Germans. Immediately all men were executed; women and children were taken to a camp, and after a week they were transported to the Auschwitz concentration camp. Anusia, who was a small-built girl, somehow managed to squeeze between trash cans that were driven from the Pruszkow camp to a nearby dump, and she escaped by jumping off the truck as it was going through a small forest. The baby survived in spite of severe bruises and cuts. Not having a place to go to, Anusia stayed with me. We found an old mattress somewhere and she made her bed on the floor right next to mine. I shared all I had with her, since all she had was what she carried on her back.

After Anusia's arrival others came, and their stories were just as horrible. And so the refugee crowd poured in until Christmas. The population in our apartment doubled. Some of our relatives came just to die there, others after a short stay managed to find better quarters. The Germans were still there, but everyone knew they had lost the war; the Allies and freedom were just around the corner.

We could hear the rumble of heavy artillery and even

sometimes the rattle of machine guns. The Germans started to evacuate, and life was in a state of chaos in the city. The Nazis were stealing whatever they could from the Poles, and the Poles were stealing all they could from the Nazis.

Truck after truck was going west, filled with Polish art collections, paintings, furniture, and other items of value. And we all were raiding the German food stores, now left open and deserted. One time I managed to get, before others snatched them, two big bags of noodles, some lard, and some coffee.

Weisenbek, before leaving his place, called on Uncle Stefan and said that all that was left in the apartment was for us to take and use.

The Nazis had left a small garrison to cover their retreat, but the Soviets had surrounded the city, and many Germans were caught inside. The Red ring grew tighter, the roar of guns was very loud, and finally the Soviets were there. They came first through our street creeping along the walls like a mass of gray locusts. They looked hungry, ragged, but they crept on and on.

Then came carts drawn by small shaggy horses. People stood, looked, and wondered. Some prepared to greet the Russians, others shook their heads, saying we would be sorry the Germans had left. The Reds used a few planes, but people did not run for shelter; only a few bombs fell. The garrison was wiped out very quickly, and that was the end of the Germans in Krakow. The only remaining German I saw was the corpse of an unknown soldier left on the bank of the river. The first time I saw the body, it was fully dressed, face-down on the ground. The next, someone had rolled him over, exposing his face, mouth half open, a dark stain of frozen blood on his cheek. His shoes, coat, and jacket had been removed. Today, completely naked, his blue eyes stare out of his twisted face. I stop to look. Who is he? Without his uniform he no longer looks German. Does he have a family? Is his mother waiting for him to return home? He is young, perhaps not as old as I. Momentary pity is replaced by loathing. I remember the death and destruction that he and his kind have inflicted on my family, my country.

"Well, Mr. Nazi, how does it feel, here, now, and like this? Where is your power, your master race?"

Two young boys hear me. They are gaunt, ragged, with noses red from the frosty wind. Their clothing, many sizes too small, was outgrown years ago. Their pant legs, ending inches above their ankles, and their wooden shoes, without socks, leave purple bracelets of naked legs. The sleeves of their jackets reach just below the elbows and have two additions sewed onto them, different colors, but long enough to pull over their frozen fingers. They look like clowns from the circus.

We are all clowns these days, in a sad circus. One of the boys comes closer to the German body, bends over him, and spits in his face.

"You hate this dead man?" I ask.

"Sure, he was a German, in uniform until two days ago, son of a bitch."

"But he is dead!"

"No, he is not dead, he is a German."

The other boy bends over, clears his throat, and spits

at the face. They leave; their revenge is young. It takes a long time to learn how to hate. Watching the two clowns as they leave the stage, I cannot applaud. I'm afraid, afraid of what is in me. Half ashamed, not wanting anyone to see me, I look at the naked body, shiver, close my eyes, then spit at him.

"He is not dead. He is a German!"

Part Three

THE
RUSSIANS

═══ RUSSIANS TAKE WARSAW, ═══ REPORTED IN CRACOW

War News Summarized

Warsaw, the first European capital to fall to Hitler's blitzkrieg five years and four months ago, was liberated by Russian and Polish troops yesterday. The First White Russian Army captured the city. . . .

The Red Army steamroller, which at its closest point was 260 miles from Berlin, moved north to the Polish capital when the Second White Russian Army, from its two bridgeheads across the Narew River, advanced twenty-four miles on a sixty-two mile front, freeing Makow, Pultusk, Clechanow and 500 other communities.

At the southern end of the long surging line the First Ukrainian Army liberated Czestochowa, Radomsko and 700 more inhabited places, and Lublin reported that Cracow had also fallen. . . .

The Warsaw victory brought to a climax the diplomatic impasse over recognition of a single Polish Government by all the Allies. The Polish Government in London indicated it would seek an early return to Warsaw and the Moscow-fostered Lublin regime was expected to move into the capital immediately.

The New York Times, *January 18, 1945*

JANUARY 1945

"Come on, time to join the party."

We stroll casually from Johnny's current home, Weisenbek's apartment, to the monastery, where Father Jan greets us in the rectory. Several monks attend to a table piled with cheese, sausage, and cakes, while others open bottles of wine long kept in their own cellar. The Allied soldiers formerly hidden in this religious community have shed their habits. Tonight they sport reddened cheeks and blurry eyes. Unrestrained by the presence of true holy men, their loosened tongues repeat crude jokes.

After I have enjoyed several glasses of wine and kissed each of the soldiers goodbye (some more than once!), I kiss three of the monks. They do not resist, but Father Jan soon reproaches me. "Christine, I prefer that you shake hands with my monks."

A life-size effigy of Adolf Hitler is held up for all to see.

"Hang him, hang him." Our shouts echo through the room. Johnny lifts a friend to his shoulder and then a second, who throws a rope over the high crossbeam. Adolf Hitler swings through the air. We spit, hurl obscenities, and pummel with our fists. The monks who witness our flailing grin with approval.

When the frenzy subsides, Johnny, waving for silence, raises his glass. "To you, my friends, to Father Jan, to all of you who have risked your lives to save ours—to each of you, thank you. We shall not forget."

My eyes half fill with tears. Perhaps I have had too much.

∎ ∎ ∎

We find that the whole city is celebrating, and we join a group of people who are tearing down swastikas, ripping up portraits of Hitler. Johnny, accustomed to hiding, is alarmed by this raucous upheaval, where drunken Poles as well as Russians dance in the streets.

We furtively observe the Red Army, the soldiers who have "liberated" us. With their long mustaches, slanting eyes, and yellow complexions, they seem more like the armies of Genghis Khan than our notion of liberators.

That evening there is no curfew and people roam the streets all night long. The Russians have found some vodka supplies, and as the night wears on, more and more of them get drunk. They invade private houses, raping, shooting, destroying everything they can. The results of their looting are apparent the next day, as they parade about in all kinds of civilian clothes stolen from Polish families, looking like tramps in garments that do not fit.

Watches hold a great fascination for them—it is dangerous to wear a watch these days. The Russians brandish pistols and shout *"Dawaj czasy."* (Give the watch.) You see soldiers walking down the street with an alarm clock hanging around their neck or a collection of wristwatches on each arm.

One day Aunt Krystyna and I are met in our gateway by a drunken Russian soldier. He blocks our path, pointing his rifle directly at us. When I try to reason with him to let us pass, he hits me with the barrel of his gun, pushes me into a corner, then starts hitting the wall with his rifle butt, the barrel still pointing at me. Knowing how easily the gun could go off, I remove my watch and dangle it in front of his face. "Damned whores," he growls, grabbing the watch, then reels into the street.

People begin to disappear suddenly, and no one knows why, or where they are taken. No one feels safe on the streets. Like a drop of fresh water in the ocean, once they fall out of sight, they are never seen again.

=== THE NEW POLAND ===
RUSSIAN-MADE REGIME SEEKS TO REBUILD A RUINED COUNTRY

The first complete picture record of Poland to be obtained in six years. . . . In Poland [photographer] Phillips found devastation but not despair. Only 80,000 of Poland's 3,500,000 Jews remained. There were still 100,000 bodies in the ruins of Warsaw. Some 10,000 Poles were dying every month of tuberculosis. And 5,000,000 of the country's 25,000,000 people still had to find homes. Only a quarter of Poland's livestock remained. But the new government had started schools, hospitals, cinemas and houses of culture. It had distributed the great landlords' estates among the peasants. It had organized unions. It had taken over the nation's hotels, mines, steel mills, public utilities, harbors and most of the food distribution, leaving the small businesses and the small farms in the hands of their owners.

Behind the facade of the government, the will of Moscow was still decisive in Poland. There were said to be as many as 80,000 political prisoners held in concentration camps. The press was technically free but the news came from the government news service, Polpress. There was no real freedom of speech. There was mysterious nightly shooting in the streets. Government leaders condemned all opposition to them as "reactionary" or "fascist." The Red Army was leaving Poland but it was taking great herds of cattle with it.

All Poland was suffering from a lingering case of psychic shock.

Life, *November 19, 1945*

FEBRUARY 1945

Then one day in the middle of February came the coup de grace, Yalta, the agreement that buried our hopes once and for all.

All of Poland had waited while Roosevelt, Churchill, and Stalin bargained our fate at Yalta. We had supposed that the occupation of Poland would be momentary, that when the war was finally over the Russians would return to Russia and Poland would be free again.

"It is finished. We are to be a feast for the Russian wolves. The cards have been played. We belong to the

Russians," Uncle Stefan shouts, entering the room where we huddle in our extra sweaters, trying to keep warm.

Was it for this that we had fought and died on the streets, in prisons, and in concentration camps? Is it for this that our cities are lying in ruins? Is it for this that our soldiers and pilots were fighting and dying side by side with the Allied forces on all the western fronts?

It was the first time I ever saw my mother cry.

The Russians open the gates of Auschwitz. Ella and I, part of a Red Cross team, reach the camp after traveling five hours on a road ruined by tanks, German and Russian. We continually detour around columns of Russian troops, who call out obscene invitations.

"Don't eat," Ella cautions. "If what I have been told is true, you'll throw up your insides. Well, let's see what we have been hearing about for three years."

ARBEIT MACHT FREI (Work Makes You Free), the sign that bears one of the most dreaded slogans in Poland, looms above us over the main gate.

Block after block of skeletons, some alive, some dead, lie side by side. Occasionally one of them groans, reaches out. Open eyes stare, compelling a hypnotic fascination.

I climb a high hill of snow to peer down at sickening devastation that would make even the wolves howl in shame. Then my foot slips, scraping the surface snow from the rubbish. A child's face gazes back at me, then two, three—it is a mound of slaughtered children.

For five days I have been struggling to blur, to close

those eyes, but I can't. They follow me at work in the hospital, where hundreds of refugees and prisoners suffer dysentery, spotted fever, gangrene, black death.

This time back at Auschwitz I don't vomit, but work as fast as I can. There is no time to feel, when so many are dying.

The loaded Red Cross lorry has room for one more. Choosing the last one is the day's most difficult decision. Three men are huddled close together in a ditch, motionless. The first seems least likely to survive, the second is too large for me to move, so I decide to take the third, if he is alive. When I lift him, he groans; sometimes such groans are only air, bellows from a dead man's belly. After I feel a faint heartbeat, I place him on the lorry.

The overloaded truck lurches through the streets, avoiding potholes, abandoned vehicles. Every room, corner, corridor, even the entrance hall of the hospital, is filled with the wounded, the critically ill, the dying. When I manage to find my patient a corner of floor, a doctor shouts, "Why did you bother with this dead body? Get him out of here."

"But Doctor, the man is still breathing."

"Give him ten minutes." His voice is tired and sarcastic. "He will stop breathing. Get him out. He is taking time and room from those who still have a chance."

Picking up the stinking bony shell of a man, I walk toward the pile of dead bodies about to be removed for mass burial. I can't. I can't throw this breathing human— Thank God, the Red Cross truck is still outside. I ask the driver to take the two of us to my parents' apartment. He gapes at me, then at the corpse I hold in my arms, shakes his head in disbelief, but agrees.

"Christine, who is he?" Mama asks.

"I don't know. They wanted me to throw him on the pile of dead. He is still breathing."

We rid him of the lice and vermin that crawl all over him. After washing him, we lay him on thick papers in the hallway and give him a few drops of water, then cover him with a warm blanket. I lean over and say, "Goodbye, stranger. I am sure you won't be with us tomorrow, but at least you are protected from cold and harm. There is nothing more that we can do for you. May you die in peace. You're entitled to that."

The unnamed stranger has been in our apartment for almost ten days. He takes a small amount of the broth Mama and Aunt Krystyna made. We have bathed and bandaged his sores and put him in cold water when his fever rose. He is able to close his eyes now, and to groan, but he does not speak. Perhaps, like a frightened animal, he is not sure if we will rescue or devour him.

The Resistance is in as much danger now as it was when the Nazis held Krakow. Soviets arrested each member of the underground who came forward at Russian request. A sinister game is being played. A number of German informers now collaborate with the Russians, and together they pursue former Resistance members with renewed zeal.

All foreigners are required to register; those with wives

and children will be repatriated via Odessa and the Black Sea. To defy the order invites arrest; nonetheless, Johnny will not comply. The three British soldiers who live with him at Weisenbek's apartment decided it is less risky to register. I am at the apartment to see if I can persuade them to take some of my women friends with them. The underground has printed fake marriage licenses to help women and children escape Poland with foreign soldiers. With a great deal of jesting about their new brides, all three agree.

"I have a special bride for one of you . . . and by the way, she has three children," I say casually. I can see them looking at each other, trying to pass the buck.

The bride is Maria, who cared for Johnny when he first came to Krakow.

"Well, which one of you?"

I start to sing a French song.

> *"Ils tirent à la courte paille*
> *Ils tirent à la courte paille*
> *Pour savoir, qui serait marié . . .*
> *Pour savoir, qui serait marié . . ."*
> *(They pull the shortest straw*
> *to see who will be married.)*

They agree to the plan, each hoping not to pull the shortest straw. Davis, the youngest and the winner, sheepishly grins and explodes into song.

> *"Its a long way to Tipperary; it's a long way to go.*
> *Its a wrong thing to tickle Mary; it's the wrong thing to do."*

Great hilarity erupts as I describe their prospective brides.

Two days later, marriage certificates and identification papers in hand, I take my three "families" to the foreigners office, where they are registered, then taken to a transit camp. In a few days they will begin the long journey home. This will be the last I will ever see of them or Maria.

=== **PATTON'S TROOPS ADVANCE** ===
ON 50 MILE FRONT

Today's War News

GUAM—Marines capture main airfield on Iwo and drive across island cutting off Japanese forces in defenses around volcano at southern tip; charge down runway by 900 Japanese broken up; night attacks by enemy planes beaten off; fleet continues bombardment of island to aid ground forces in fierce fighting; Americans now control one-fourth of the eight-square-mile island.

PARIS—United States Third Army advances up two and one-half miles on 50-mile front, captures 18 German towns in two days: American Seventh Army takes five towns, moves within three and one-half miles of Saarbrücken: German counterattacks throw Canadians back in Calcar area.

MOSCOW—German high command announces Russians have scored gains in several sectors southeast of Berlin and east of Dresden indicating Reds have withstood strong counterattacks and resumed advance. Soviet troops in Breslau suburbs, garrison rejects ultimatum to surrender.

LONDON—Nine hundred Flying Fortresses hit rail yards at Nuremberg, in eighth day of air offensive against Germany following up night raids by R.A.F.

IT'S THE HIT OF THE SEASON.

St. Louis Post-Dispatch, February 20, 1945

MARCH 1945

Our stranger's name is Hans Citroën. He still has a skeletonlike appearance. Great scars, purple lines and blotches, cover his body. If someone speaks too loudly, he cowers like a scolded dog. Today a faint smile moved across his face. He is well enough to join other prisoners from Holland for the journey home.

I have a new assignment at a first-aid clinic in Katowice, west of Krakow. The underground is sending Ella to the same location. She will arrive next month.

Henri, my official underground contact, meets me near the Red Cross shelter, an old building that is nothing more than a shed. Small and wiry, Henri appears sickly, but actually he is quick, witty, with a spicy French sense of humor. His dark eyes look me over with an embarrassing vitality. He shows me the corner room where I am to live. The room, furnished with a cot and a chair, crawls with fleas and bedbugs, all apparently immune to disinfectants.

It is a great boost when Henri returns, inviting me to be his guest. He inhabits a spacious room in a private home, owned by "friends" of his who are well aware that his real work is smuggling Resistance personnel out of Poland. His connections make good food and wine continually available. After a long, elegant dinner, Henri says, "Come, sit. This is what we are to do. As you know, the NKVD [the Russian secret police] determined that all who worked in the Polish Resistance face Siberia or death. Stalin will not tolerate a Polish Poland, *merde* [shit]; he will attempt to stifle, ultimately eliminate, every attempt at national independence. *Merde*.

"The Germans will surrender any moment now; then all foreign refugees now in the transit camps will be repatriated. We will take advantage of the situation and smuggle out our men and women as refugees.

"We have managed to obtain repatriation passes directly from the Russian office, to be given to each Resistance member. They will smuggle themselves into the transit camps over the fences at night. The camps, very dark, casually guarded, receive new people from

Auschwitz every day, so the Russians have no idea of the total number.

"Timing is the important issue," Henri continues. "Surrender will bring several days of confusion, with refugees heading east and west; and *merde alors,* in that chaos we will try to get them all out safely.

"Christine, the actual purpose of your being here is to become friendly with the Russian chief of police, Andrejew. It is essential for our operation."

My first task must be to renovate the shed—on the platform between the tracks—formerly a Russian toilet. For two days I clean and scrape filth, to reduce the odor. I actually cajole the railroad workers into fixing the windows. It begins to take on the semblance of a clinic!

Henri is a marvelous help. The two of us drive to a nearby town, Hirschberg, where we loot abandoned German homes, taking chairs, tables, pots and crockery, medical supplies, even some curtains and a rug. Now the shack is not only clean, but well equipped, a pleasant place.

The chief of police presently enters the shack, scrutinizing every corner. The eyes in this cruel face never reveal what he thinks. But his conversation indicates a chink. He is fond of children. I shall learn to use that.

A line of cattle and freight cars, crammed with children, is switched to a side track behind the station. According to Chief Andrejew, it is only the first of many trainloads that will arrive from a recently liberated camp in Germany. As I pass down the line of cars, the children who peer out through the slats call to me in a jumbled cacophony of languages.

A trainman opens one of the doors, allowing the stench of urine, foulness, to escape. The waifs are filthy, sick, covered with vermin. Some wear the striped camp uniforms, which hang like torn awnings in a fierce wind; others, in rags tied with strings, are barely clothed. Their bare feet are caked in their own excrement. They fight like animals for the places closest to outside air. Many do not know their own names.

There seems no end to the suffering. Andrejew announces another train is scheduled to arrive tomorrow. I only hope the peasants continue to bring potatoes and milk. There are no clothes, no soap or towels, but the word spreads, then wagons appear, filled with clothing collected from nearby villages. Farmers bring fresh straw for bedding.

We organize a field kitchen, set aside one car as a toilet, and use another as a washroom, where each child is undressed and given a good scrubbing in a huge wooden tub filled with warm water. Their clothes are boiled and disinfected. Thank God it has not been too cold.

The children arrive like cattle, and we have to treat them almost like cattle: Scrub, feed, disinfect, and on to the next. There is no time to get attached to them.

However, a nameless boy, about five years old, has attached himself to me. We call him Jasio. Each time I return him to his car, he reappears at the shelter before I do. Today he follows me like an emaciated, whimpering puppy, begging for more food. There is no food left. When I can't stand his crying any longer, I turn to Chief Andrejew, who is always in the shelter enjoying the nurses.

"Look, instead of bothering us, why don't you find some food for this kid?"

Andrejew grumbles, but does leave, only to reappear with a large loaf of bread and a whole round of sausage. He flings them on the mattress under the table where Jasio has hidden himself, then dashes back out before I can say a word. Jasio eats, an expression of infinite bliss on his face.

A well-fed peasant woman with a bleeding nose pushes through the door, crying. "Oh, nurse, that man, that horrible Russian bandit. He took everything I had. I carried bread and sausage to sell, and I need the money."

I glance at the two stick feet under the table, then back at the robust woman standing before me. I wash her bruises while talking loudly and continuously the entire time, in hopes that she won't hear Jasio munching.

"It's a good thing he didn't kill you. Be thankful you have your life; you'd better go before he finds you here and makes more trouble for you."

I persuade Andrejew to take Jasio for a ride on his motorcycle. The Russian obviously likes the little boy, so I am not afraid to let him go. Watching the two of them in the distance, I must remember someday Andrejew's weakness for children may help us all.

Tatek is here. This morning the door to the ambulatory ward opened and there he was! I show him the clinic and then my living quarters.

"Come, Christine, this will not do. We shall find the Piotrowskis."

Owners of a coal business, the Piotrowskis and their two daughters live in a beautiful house in the finest section of Katowice. When Tatek describes my living accommodations, they invite me to stay with them, and Ella as well. We are to share large adjoining bedrooms. I mention Johnny, hoping that Mr. Piotrowski will offer another invitation: He is to have a room on the lower floor. Wonderful!

My father and I have dinner in a restaurant, which, though it is small, boasts magnificent prewar menus.

"Tatek, choose what you wish. Tonight you are my guest."

He is surprised.

"Are you sure you have sufficient money? The prices are steep and I am rather short myself right now."

"Of course, don't worry. I earn a good salary at the clinic."

"How much do you earn?"

"Tatek, that is my secret."

Tatek orders for both of us. We will start with fried

chicken, he tells the waiter, knowing how much I love it.

"Sorry, sir, we do not have it."

"Well then, let's try the beef Bourguignon."

"Sorry sir, we do not have it."

"Wiener schnitzel?"

"Sorry sir, we do not have it."

"Well, what in hell do you have?" Tatek retorts angrily.

"Cabbage and horsemeat."

I timidly ask the price. When the waiter replies, I nudge Tatek's foot, whispering, "Order one dinner for both of us."

"Don't worry, Christine, I will pay this time. Save your fabulous salary for our next treat."

It is not important that the food, unsuccessfully camouflaged with herbs and spices, is served in a less than elegant fashion. Tatek and I spend two marvelous hours talking, laughing, remembering. My father has become old and gray. There is so little left for him, but today we have been truly happy.

I hold his arm at the station, waiting for the train. His shoulders stoop. I think about our year in Warsaw, the racetracks and the restaurants. Was it a dream? Tatek is no longer the center of attention, the wealthy friend of so many, inviting and invited. When the train stops at the platform, there is a rush for space. I hug my father, kiss him, hold him for an extra moment, and let go.

There are children to be cared for, another train tomorrow, then another two days after that.

■ ■ ■

Johnny and Ella have arrived. Neither needed to be written to twice.

═══ ALL GERMANS SURRENDER ═══
TO THREE MAJOR ALLIES

LONDON, ENGLAND (AP)—The greatest war in history ended Monday with the unconditional surrender of Germany.

The surrender of the Reich to the western Allies and Russia was made at General Eisenhower's headquarters at Reims, France, by Col. Gen. Gustav Jodl, chief of staff for the German army.

The news came in an Associated Press dispatch from Reims. Earlier German broadcasts told the German people that Grand Admiral Karl Doenitz had ordered the capitulation of all fighting forces, and called off the U-boat war. . . .

The end of the European warfare, greatest, bloodiest and costliest war in human history— at least 40,000,000 casualties on both sides in killed, wounded and captured—came after five years, eight months and six days of strife that overspread the globe.

Hitler's armies invaded Poland on September 1, 1939, beginning the agony that convulsed the world for 2,076 days. . . .

The BBC said telephone conversations were going on between London, Washington and Moscow in order to fix the exact hour of the V-E day announcement by President Truman, Prime Minister Churchill and Premier Stalin.

The Milwaukee Journal, *May 7, 1945*

MAY 8, 1945 VE DAY

There are no celebrations when the Germans surrender. We defeated them but lost the war. The German surrender signifies the transfer from one oppressor to another.

Henri is excited but tense. "For many this is the last opportunity for freedom and safety. We must have the first transport ready to leave, without knowing which day that will be."

He transmits messages to thirty of the most desperate; they must assemble at his apartment in three days.

Johnny, when he is restless, can be a pest. Now, on the Piotrowskis' balcony, he informs me we are missing a great celebration in New Zealand and in London. He craves a party, then imagines my going with him to his "land of eternal spring."

I only want freedom for my country. "Look at you, untouched by the war. You stayed in a warm monastery and ate well. Often you couldn't even stand the boredom of your safe hiding place, so at the risk of *our* lives we had to arrange parties to keep *you* from breaking down. You made love to me as if no other loyalties mattered.

"I have seen too many dead, too many wounded, too many starved and crazed. I see my father broken and my mother's tears. You will go home, and all that you left there will be safe, intact. Your only scars will be a few scratches inside yourself. And I? . . . Where is home now? What have the Russians done to Adampol? Looted? Divided? What the Germans did not destroy, the Russians will. No, Johnny, for you it is over; for me it can never end."

=== **POLAND** ===
Plagiarism

The Lublin radio, in a Yiddish broadcast, announced last week that it had been decided to create a camp for Germans "and members of the German ethnic group" in the former Warsaw ghetto. The camp would be a "place of isolation on which everybody would look with disgust, a place to house those who wanted to murder and rape the entire world, a camp for men who have no right to the name of man but should be called beasts."

Time, *May 28, 1945*

MAY 25, 1945

Henri notified the thirty Resistance officers, judges, and aristocrats. When they arrive in Katowice, some with their families, the original number doubles. They fear for their lives, as most of them are on the Russian suspect list. Repatriation passes, meticulously detailed to match other official French refugee passes, are distributed.

The hundreds of authentic refugees, mostly ex-prisoners from the concentration camps, suffer from acute malnutrition. Language is the real difficulty. Henri, assuming the role of leader for all French and Belgian refugees, speaks on their behalf with the Russian authorities. They offer Henri the use of an ex-German military camp five miles west of Katowice. Primitive, but surprisingly adequate, it is clean, with bunkbeds, straw mattresses, several electric lights, running water, and bathrooms. It is surrounded by a barbed-wire fence. Six Russian soldiers stand guard at its sole entrance. They never patrol, but rely on their dogs, untrained hungry mongrels, to guard the camp. By May fifteenth the camp is stretched to its limits with the Russian-approved refugees.

The first dark night, under the cover of a foggy drizzle, after midnight, we approach the camp with our own refugees. Adults carry their children, who have been drugged so they will not cry. Henri conveys a cat in a bag, which he lets out as the watchdogs come toward us. Barking and baying, they chase the cat across the field, the six Russians sleepily stumbling out of the shed and attempting to follow. Our refugees quickly slither into the camp.

The transport officer will reveal to us neither the date nor time of departure, so we become more nervous each day. There is the ever-threatening possibility of an informer among us who will recognize one of our people or become aware of the children, who speak Polish rather than French.

Our most serious undertaking is acquiring clearance passes from the NKVD allowing passage across the Polish-Czech border. The NKVD requires a valid reason and is suspicious of everyone. Escape to the American zone is a criminal act; the slightest suspicion brings imprisonment.

Ella and I rehearse our official story, then often repeat it back to each other.

"Are you afraid?" I ask.

"Why should I be? The NKVD, being more stupid than I am, will never guess the truth. Just smile, wink at them—"

"Ella, I don't think flirting will do any good. Our new names—Krystyna Wieczorek, Ella Bielec—the possibility that someone might recognize us, frightens me."

"How could anyone? We have had these names since we came to Katowice. It will go smoothly."

"I hope you're right—"

"Here, put some lipstick on; the Russkies like it!"

The soldier at the desk, efficient, polite, escorts us to an adjacent office, where he points to the officer he thinks will be most responsive. The officer listens, informs us he has no authority to issue such passes, and directs us to a third man, a civilian.

He questions us, first together, then separately. His questions are penetrating and sarcastic.

"Why should two pretty girls like you be so interested in sick refugees?"

Satisfied with our answers, smiling, in a good-natured tone he says, "You can go, but I will give you only a short pass, one week."

Ella pleads, "The trains run rather slow in these times, and we might need ten days."

"All right, ten days," he responds, signing the two passes while placing his official seal on each.

I must tell Johnny what I am doing and insist he leave on the first transport to Czechoslovakia. In my room at the Piotrowskis' Johnny starts to kiss me, but I push him away.

"Sit down and have a cigarette. I have something serious to say to you."

"We can be serious later."

"No, Johnny, now. These transports endanger my life. If the Russians catch me, you will be in graver danger than you are. It is time for you to leave Poland."

"For Christ's sake, Christine, what are you involved in?"

His face darkens while I tell him.

"You are a damn fool. You know what these bastards will do if they catch you. No matter how much you insist, I will not leave you, and I won't go to the American zone unless you come with me ... and bullshit to your protests."

Angrily I taunt, "Do you have a brain? If they catch me, do you really think you could help? Talk to them in English, perhaps? You are making a target of yourself, imperiling the Piotrowskis."

"Don't shout at me, and stop arguing. If they catch

you I will go on a rampage and shoot every damn Russian in sight until they kill me."

"That's clever. You would kill four Commies, get yourself killed, and bury me."

My temper unleashed, I slam the door behind me and storm down the stairs. Still furious, I run into Henri.

"Calm down, Christine. How do you argue with a man in love? You should know better—well, perhaps you are not old enough."

"I am old enough! And I don't want *him* to be in love with me!"

Henri, asserting his French comprehension of such problems, assures me that he is an expert in affairs of the heart and will be an intermediary with Johnny.

"Fine! Be sure that he is on the first train to Czecho-slovakia."

Henri has recruited half a dozen prostitutes. "I must know if they can be trusted to help us. I think they are loyal Poles, but I must be sure. It is a dangerous business with these girls, for you never know if they will sell themselves to a higher bidder."

"I'm nineteen. How am I supposed to find out such things?"

"Some are younger than you. Talk to them, try to sense their hearts, if they are more Polish than the appetites of their bodies."

Henri is a good judge of Polish women. They may sell themselves, but not their country. The ladies will be transported to the Polish-Czech border town to engage the border police while our train leaves Poland.

■ ■ ■

Andrejew has sent word that a refugee train, waiting on a side track, will leave for Czechoslovakia in three hours. To avoid stowaways, the Russians have kept the information secret until this very moment. The train must be loaded now.

There is little time to move the refugees from the camp five miles away. A few trucks are available for the sick and very old, but the rest will have to walk, and walk fast. Our food and medical supplies are in a warehouse a mile from the station, and that too will have to be carried by hand.

Exhausted, we collapse on the train after everyone is on board. Among the refugees there is at least one person who should not be here, an Alsatian, still dressed in his German uniform and near death from smallpox. We tried to persuade the police that he should be hospitalized, but they would not hear of it and ordered him onto the train.

The Russians padlock the doors to the long line of freight cars containing the refugees. Ella, Henry, and I stretch out in a passenger car, empty except for the three of us. Just out of sight of the station, Henri explodes. "*Merde,* the Russians didn't give me the keys to the cars."

The train moves at such a snail's pace, one can hop on and off and easily catch up. Ella and I lie in the sun on the platform car behind our passenger car, soaking up all the warmth we can. Late in the afternoon we stop at a village, where Henri gets off to consult with the train engineer. They come and tell us to go back to the passenger compartment. A moment later Henri returns in a truck housing his harem, which is driven onto the platform car. The journey continues.

At dusk, Henri halts the train to let the refugees out of the freight cars to use the natural "roadside facilities." As the Russians have not given him keys, he again confers with the engineer, who deftly uses an ax, sending the padlocks into the bushes. The refugees come out of the cars, shadowy night figures, disappear into the underbrush, then return. Like ghostly stars, only their eyes show up in the twilight.

Each adult refugee is given rations: a parcel containing a piece of bread, a tablespoon of marmalade, and half an inch of sausage. In addition, every child is given a cup of milk. We advise them to eat slowly, perhaps over several hours, as there will be no additional food until the same time tomorrow.

Now that the sun is down it is getting cold on the platform car, so Henri invites his prostitutes to make themselves comfortable in the various compartments of our passenger car. He disappears to entertain his flock and we hear his laughter move from compartment to compartment.

It is impossible to sleep in this crawling, jolting train that stops every few miles. The refugees, no longer locked in their cars, climb in and out, shouting to each other, wanting to know where we are and how much longer. No one can tell them; we don't know. At sunrise we stop again. Henri emerges from his seraglio and again consults with the engineer.

They return to the flatbed car to unload the truck. Henri kisses, hugs, and pats each of his six girls as they climb noisily on the truck to perch upon six cases of vodka. Waving his arms, Henri shouts *"À bientôt"* as they pull away.

The Czech border is nearby, Henri informs us, but we will have to wait at least two hours until the girls have had a chance to get involved in their work. We make the rounds of the freight cars, Ella speaking in Polish and I in French. She tells our Polish people to remain in the cars during the entire border procedure, pretending to be either sick or asleep, and above all to be sure that each child is given the sleeping pill she distributes for each one. Our greatest danger is the accidental cry of a Polish child.

"Do not open the doors until we tell you. If the Russians open the doors, do not come out unless someone speaks to you in French. Remember, you are all *French* citizens and you do not speak Russian or Polish!"

It is our final admonition as we close the doors on the thin, tired faces looking back at us. The closing of such doors in recent years has meant a journey toward the concentration camp, the gas chamber, certain death. This time, with some luck, it may be a journey to freedom.

It is eleven A.M. on the border between Poland and Czechoslovakia. An empty railroad platform greets Henri as he approaches the border guard's office. He suggests we ask a few of the real refugees to get out of the cars and mingle on the station platform. We are about to tell them when, winking, he reappears with all the passports, a sign that all is well.

Four Russians emerge from their office with five prostitutes clinging to their necks. They wave Henri away, shouting "shit" and "bugger off." We clamber back into the cars, hug each other, and "bugger off" as quickly as we can. The train, traveling so sluggishly before, now whisks through the Czech countryside. Tired, jubilant, Henri looks as though he could sleep standing up.

"*Merde*, I think I'll get some sleep."

"Henri, before you sleep . . . the Alsatian with smallpox is dead. What should we do with him?" I ask.

"*Merde alors*, we must get rid of him."

"How?"

"I'll shove him off!"

Like a monkey he climbs from car to car until he reaches the one with the Alsatian. He opens the side door. Leaning out the window, farther ahead I see the body thrown from the car, rolling down the slope into the ditch. Back in the compartment, Henri soon falls asleep on the opposite bench.

Prague, Czechoslovakia. The train slows and jerks to a side track outside Prague, where a railway official tells us to remain until trucks come to take us to the refugee camp. There we will receive food and, in two days, papers allowing us to cross the border into the American zone. We pass the word to the refugees, who without complaint and with a bit more patience understand they will reach the end, freedom, a return to home or to a new life. By midmorning the trucks arrive and we are driven to the camp, a huge building that once was a school.

After hot showers, warm food, and clean clothes, all provided by the Red Cross, we are summoned to Red Cross headquarters, which is also a police office. Investigators, in civilian clothes, exude politeness but ask provocative questions. For Henri and Ella it is simple; Henri speaks only French and Ella only Polish. Several investigators examine my pass, noting that my identity is as both nurse and interpreter. Suspicion aroused, they question faster than I can answer.

"Where did you learn English? French? What schools did you attend? Why did you learn languages? Are you French? Have you ever been out of Poland? Where? Are you sure?"

Thinking fast, fabricating answers to fit my new identity, I tell them that as a little girl I heard people speak in different languages, that it fascinated me. I learned them as a hobby.

At first they thought I was a spy; in Russia only spies speak foreign languages. Finally, accepting my explanation, they release all three of us, suggesting that we visit Prague. The necessary papers for the American zone will be ready in two days. As we leave the headquarters, Henri winks at me again.

"My, but you are a suspicious one . . . and clever, too. Why did you learn all those languages?"

"*Merde alors,*" I answer.

Ella has no interest in going to Prague with Henri

and me. During the transport she befriended a Belgian lawyer and wants to go out with him and have a good time. How they enjoy each other is beyond my comprehension. The only word she knows in French is *merde*, which she acquired from Henri, and her Belgian lawyer comprehends not one word of Polish.

At a small cafe, Henri and I sip wine outside in the sun, listening to tzigane music played by a gypsy violinist. There is no conversation between us until Henri asks if I want to go with him.

"Thanks, no. I want to be by myself for a while."

I walk the banks of the River Vltava, delighting in the beauty of Prague, now and then kicking a stone, smiling at a stranger. A tiredness overpowers me. I want nothing more than a soft, clean bed.

Henri's shouting at the door, something about "only one of us," awakens me. The sun indicates I have slept till noon.

"Only one nurse will be allowed on the transport to the American zone," Henri states as I open the door for him and Ella. She looks desolate, an appearance I attribute to her being madly in love with her Belgian lawyer and wanting to go to the American zone to be with him just a little longer.

"It's no problem. I'll go back to Katowice and wait for you. One should never stand in the way of love," I tell them sarcastically. It is a mystery to me how Ella falls in and out of love so often.

On the next train to Katowice, I have a compartment to myself with no lights to separate me from the outside darkness. Hands behind my head, I lean back, stretch my legs across to the opposite seat, and reflect about Ella and her Belgian, but more about Henri. In three months my understanding of him has grown. He loves money, has no scruples, cheats for fun, and kills without remorse. His pleasures include women, drink, and most exciting of all, diabolical plots—against Germans, Russians, individual enemies, it doesn't matter. He once bragged to me that during the German occupation, long before I knew him, he blew up German transports, trains moving to the Russian front. He sold tickets to young people who wanted to watch, proud of what he called a very good business, since there were many warped people who wanted to see German bodies exploding in a thousand pieces.

Henri needs women as he needs food and drink. His affairs are like his thin dark mustache, which changes as often as his character. Today he has one, tomorrow it's gone. I acknowledge that I don't really like him, actually feel disgust for him, but we are bound together in a cause which makes me admire all the wrong qualities in him, for they are essential to our current task. I admire his courage, because I am so often frightened. He laughs in the face of danger and dismisses it. He is good to me, compassionate, even tender. It is unusual for him to like or respect a woman, and sometimes I think—

The train jolts me awake. We are nearing Katowice, going back. I was so close to Czechoslovakia and freedom that going back seems like imprisonment. First it was the Germans, then Johnny, then the Russians, then the underground, all of them telling me what to do—people of rank and power ordering me around, sometimes even my own mind ordering me to do what my emotions rebel against. I don't want to give up a single inch of my freedom!

Johnny is a mistake, possessive and domineering. I shall not marry him. Someday I will find someone. . . .

This morning I am in Krakow saying goodbye to all my family. I tell them that I will leave Poland with Johnny. For hours I tried to persuade Jerome to leave Poland too, to go west to freedom, but he will hear none of it. Only Uncle Stefan seems to understand. He gives me a letter of introduction to a friend in Prague, Count Schönborn. They were at school together in Vienna. Mama is her reserved self, sad and worried about my reputation.

"People will talk about you. It is just not the thing to do."

"Reputation?" I think, how ridiculous, you should worry about my life. "Mama, it won't be easy abroad, but I will never forget you. I will send help to you as soon as I can."

She hugs me, making a sign of the cross with her thumb on my forehead . . . whispering, "May God protect you."

Tatek offers encouragement. "Christine, now that you are on your own, wherever you go in the West, you will have to be totally responsible for yourself. There will be no family to help, but you have great courage and I wish you well."

Tatek, my wonderful father from Adampol and Warsaw, so young and flamboyant, now an old man, takes
me in his arms. I tell him, "You will see, someday we
will live together in a free country away from all this
pain."

Uncle Stefan holds me the longest. Fully aware of my
involvement with the transports, fearful of the danger
until they are over, I can tell by his hug that he deeply
loves me. "Be careful, Christine. I trust you, know that
you will do well, and rejoice for your life in a free
country. You've earned it!"

I think about that first journey, from my home to
Krakow. Then I had had to leave my horses, my rabbit,
my pets behind. Now, starting a new life once more, I
have to leave my closest family.

Holding back tears, I rush to the train to get back to
Katowice, Henri, Ella, and the next transport.

Ella proclaims the most intimate details of her latest
love.

"I am madly in love, and he has promised to marry
me. Only one more transport, and I am going to Belgium
to marry him and live with him forever."

"Ella, Ella, slow down. How do you know he proposed
marriage? You can't understand a word he says."

"Oh, it was quite easy. As we were visiting one of the
churches in Pilsen, he hugged me and sang the wedding
march."

What can one say? . . . only share her joy.

Henri opens a bottle of fine French wine. He, Johnny, Ella, and I drink to each of our journeys to freedom.

"To Ella and the Belgian!"

"To Johnny and Christine!"

"To Henri and his women by the truckload!"

The pain of parting is momentarily replaced by our thoughts of the future before us.

═ POLAND ═

Election Postponed

The U.S. and Britain had recognized Poland's Warsaw government. But of the Yalta agreement (to broaden that Government by the inclusion of democratic Poles, pending democratic national elections) little was left. The "broadened" Warsaw government was still dominated by Russia through Polish Communists and fellow travelers. Last week the election promise was deferred. Premier Edward Osubka-Morawski announced that he, personally, would like to see an election soon but "until harvesting, repatriation and resettlement are finished, we must not divert attention from these basic tasks." Since repatriation and resettlement involve several million people, the Polish election was in effect indefinitely postponed.

Time, *July 23, 1945*

JUNE 1945

This second transport may look on the surface like the first, but there the resemblance ceases. We depart from the same camp, carry the same truckload of whores and the vodka. However the number of Polish refugees has increased, and so has their luggage. Huge wooden crates, rolled-up oriental carpets, and a profusion of trunks abound. Henri laughs at me for questioning the luggage. Angered, I shout, "Do you think they are all fools? No one will believe that people from the concentration camp could possess such things. It is a miracle if they have adequate clothing, but oriental rugs? Henri, what the hell are you going to do if the Russian police investigate?"

Henri continues to laugh, waving an envelope full of money at me. These "refugees" aren't persecuted by the NKVD. They are wealthy people who want to leave Poland to start a new life in a free country, and Henri takes this opportunity to make some money by getting them out. He charges an exorbitant sum. Even worse, he has spread the word he will take anyone out who can afford his price.

I am livid. I will risk my life to help those truly persecuted by the Russians, but why should I be killed for oriental rugs? I, too, hope to find freedom one day, but not at the cost of other people's safety.

Johnny says that he has suspected all along that Henri's noble evacuation of refugees and Resistance personnel is really a cover for his greed. "You are an idealistic fool, Christine. Henri will look after himself, no one else!"

There is nothing I can do. The train loaded, we start for the American zone in Pilsen. I cease complaining as Henri, Johnny, and I spend most of the twenty-four hours playing poker. Henri loses a fortune to us and *that* makes the time go faster.

One of the whores, Zofia, takes a special liking to me. She assists with the passengers, distributing food and lending a hand to mothers with their children. Quiet, intelligent, with a warm heart, she knew early on what the transports were all about. Henri, by a slip of the tongue, tells her my real name. She excitedly relates that her parents were employed on my cousin's estate and that when the Germans arrested them, it was my cousin who arranged and paid for her release.

"I will never forget his kindness," she concludes.

Zofia has a kind of adoration for me and can't restrain herself from calling me Countess, though I beg her repeatedly not to.

Arriving at the border town, the scene replicates last time: half-dressed women, drunken Russian soldiers, empty vodka bottles on the platform. Henri, having gotten off the train earlier and onto the trucks with the prostitutes, is waiting there for us.

I turn to Johnny. "Say your prayers, this is it."

"Don't worry, I'm always lucky. Nothing will happen to us."

"But look, Henri's not smiling. He's in a bad mood. Something went wrong."

Johnny says he probably had one too many with the Russians, but I know better. Henri never drinks at moments like this. I jump down from the car.

"There is trouble ahead. *Merde alors*. There are two very sober NKVD men in the station building waiting to check all our papers."

Behind the desk, two men await us. They do not rise. They address Henri in impeccable French, then speak to me in perfect Polish. I have already noticed that they spoke fluent Russian to the border guards. They introduce themselves so quickly I cannot catch their full names, only Colonel, Major, and one surname that began with "Rose." I am certain they are educated Jews, but I am unsure of their original nationality. Their knowledge of three languages, their witty yet precise questioning, their sense of history and awareness of national struggles affirm their education.

For two hours we struggle under their questioning, at first together, then separately. Continually smiling, their faces never indicate pleasure or displeasure. The same question is asked four or five times, each in different contexts. At last they are satisfied.

Many people from the transport have come out of the cars despite Henri's orders to remain inside. The angry Russian soldiers yell "Get the hell out of here" and threaten us with their rifles. Back on the train, we hear the doors close, but we do not move. The wait, probably only fifteen minutes, seems like months.

When the train finally starts, we utter our first words.

"Ella missed all the excitement," I utter, trying to ease the tension.

"She would have loved it," retorts Johnny sarcastically. Ella didn't come on this transport, for she wanted to return to Krakow, wind up her affairs, and leave Poland on the third transport to join her Belgian lawyer.

Happy about our luck, we settle back into our poker game to give Henri a chance to win back some of his fortune. My concentration is interrupted by my recurring thoughts of the two officers who have just interrogated us. I feel they would not have hesitated to send us to a concentration camp or death. Were they really Jews? Don't they know about Auschwitz? I sip my wine, play my cards, but can't get them out of my mind.

Two Polish refugees interrupt, speaking to Henri in Polish while I translate.

"Mr. Henri, there are two strangers on the train. We did not notice when they came on board but they were not here when we left Katowice."

"Are you positive?"

"Oh yes, we all recognize each other. These two are not from this transport, as they speak several languages and ask too many questions."

"What are they asking? What do they say?"

"They say that they are refugees, but I do not believe it."

"You stay here. Do not leave this compartment," Johnny orders as he and Henri stand up to leave.

I start counting telephone poles, as I did in childhood when traveling with Mama or Tatek . . . two poles . . . ten poles . . . a hundred . . . two hundred.

Johnny and Henri return. I notice a red smudge on Henri's right hand, dealing cards as if nothing has happened. There is a terrible silence; they play poker grimly, not speaking. I can't bear the silence any longer.

"Johnny, what happened?"

"They didn't like the ride, so they got off." Henri's response is casual.

"We killed them and dumped them out," Johnny tells me grimly. "Now let's finish the poker game and as soon as the train slows down or stops at a small station we are getting out."

I can't believe it, wonder how they killed them, then feel lucky I wasn't part of it. But I *am* part of it. Everyone on the train is in this together, and the double murder will jeopardize us all.

I examine my poker hand. "Give me three cards."

I win, stuff the cards in my pocket, and ask, "Now what are we going to do?"

"Spread the news immediately to the Polish refugees that there is grave danger ahead; everyone must abandon the train and seek their own way to Pilsen," Henri responds.

"What about their treasures, their rugs, their luggage?"

"*Merde!*"

"What do you mean, *merde*? You made them pay through the nose for their passage to safety."

"I took the money for getting them on the train, and I don't give a damn what happens to them from now on. And what's more, I'll charge the next batch a double fee."

At a tiny station, somewhere miles from Prague, more than twenty-five of us forsake the train to meld with the local inhabitants and disappear. Only the "real" refugees remain on board.

The train now a dot in the distance, we walk through the station to the main street, where we agree to separate and meet a mile outside of town where a large grove of trees is clearly visible. No one seems to notice me as I walk carrying only a package of food. At the trees we greet each other like friends separated for months rather than minutes.

The Czechoslovakian countryside is beautiful in June, its farmland alive and full of life. War is so full of death. Walking until sunset, we decide to have a picnic beside the road. The murders, our flight from the train, our being in Russian-occupied territory, none of these dampen our appetite or mood. We joke, eat plenty of food, and consume two bottles of wine. Tomorrow we will hitch a ride to Prague.

At the end of the day Henri finds a pile of freshly cut hay. Johnny and I lie side by side. It is not a night to make love. Henri snores while Johnny's arm falls limp around me; he too is asleep. What kind of dreams do people have, I wonder, after killing two people?

Sunrise. We must reach Prague today. Henri and Johnny send me to the road's edge as hitchhiking bait. The third truck stops and offers us a ride, the driver leaning out of his window, shouting, "Ride on the sacks back there. They have potatoes and vegetables, but you can't hurt them. There is no room in the cab."

We trade a bottle of vodka for the driver's thermos of coffee and have our breakfast, leftovers from yesterday's picnic. The driver assures us we will be in Prague by late afternoon.

■ ■ ■

The Red Cross center in Prague bustles with people. Some of the passengers who left the train where we did have arrived before us. I ask one of them, "How did you get here so fast, and where are the others?"

"Some of us have already gone to the American zone through the forest; we assume they made it."

"And your luggage?"

He smiles. "We managed!"

After a long hot shower, I search for the information center, then ask the woman there if she recognizes the name, Count Philip Schönborn. The woman at the desk hands me his address at once.

A delightful surprise, he is charming, handsome, and as Mama would say, he carries his title well. He peruses Uncle Stefan's letter, greets me with open warmth, and asks many questions about our family. I relate the sadness of Adampol's loss, the horrors of the Krakow imprisonments, and the difficulties of the Russian presence. He knows more about Uncle Stefan and Aunt Krystyna than I do. Now he frowns, troubled, as I recount my involvements with the transports and the smuggling of Polish Resistance members to the American zone.

"With spies and informers everywhere, the Russians are not as stupid as they sometimes seem. You must be very careful here. If you need help or get into trouble, try to get in touch with me, for fortunately I am acquainted with a few very important people. Enough of this, Christine. We should celebrate!"

Count Schönborn's villa, unscathed by the war, is nearly a carbon copy of my family's home before we were thrown out. Down a long gallery historic paintings hang on the walls; the floors are parquet with scattered oriental rugs; antique and modern art objects are arranged in each room with taste and elegance. Scarcely have I had time to experience the tranquillity of this home when he whisks me off to a small house just outside of Prague, where in the attic there is a miniature fashionable store.

The official stores have little stock, less style. The better prewar store owners have opened small boutiques in their homes. Outlawed under Communist rule, these unofficial places are doing a thriving business. This one is full of custom-made dresses, as well as shoes and cosmetics. Count Schönborn buys me a lovely dress and shoes then takes me to a hairdresser, which I really need.

When we finally return to the villa he exclaims, "You look beautiful. I shall call a taxicab and we shall go to dinner. I have already made the reservation."

The restaurant, occupying the entire second floor of a private villa, is also a small secret business available to a small group of people in the city. Count Schönborn, a frequent guest, greets many people in the dining room. We have a very good dinner, the best I have had in five years, and stay up late, talking and listening to music. He treats me like a queen and I really enjoy his company. It is about one o'clock in the morning when he brings me back to my hotel.

"What are you doing here so late?" Johnny both startles and accuses me. "I have been waiting for you.

Where the hell have you been? Who did you go out with tonight, and where did you manage to get this dress? I waited here all evening, hoping we would go someplace together."

"It's none of your business. Why can't you just live and let live? I owe you no explanations."

Not wanting an argument to spoil the evening's memory, I turn my back on him, enter my room, and shut the door . . . five minutes, and I am fast asleep.

We have safely crossed the border into the American zone of Czechoslovakia, the first time in six years that I have been in a free part of the world. My encounter with the Americans is exciting, confusing, and at times grating. They speak English in an accent difficult to understand, chew gum, which I have never seen before and find disgusting, and are improperly mannered. Eating chicken with their fingers, burping loudly, they even lean back and put their feet on the table. They are outgoing and friendly, sometimes too much so as they pat me on the shoulder and call me by my first name. Of course, these are only soldiers and perhaps do not represent many Americans.

Some of the Americans are Negroes. Never having seen one, I am fascinated by the shininess of their skin, their broad features, and the fact that they don't look at all like the pictures in *Uncle Tom's Cabin* I read as a child. . . . Perhaps I fear their strangeness.

Walking with Johnny toward the military office of the American intelligence, I endeavor to conceal my excitement. We are going there to report on the current situation in Poland, to persuade the Americans to absorb the transports we smuggle out, and to help our people to resettle in free countries.

The American intelligence officer, young and officious, introduces us to two others who will participate in our briefing. He asks many questions and makes clear he doesn't believe our answers. Johnny insists on detailing accounts of the Russian annihilation of the Resistance, aristocracy, and intelligentsia. In vain he attempts to communicate the desperation faced by certain Poles. The Americans smile.

"We recognize that both of you have been through a great trauma, but your imagination *must* be kept under control. We have been working with the Russians for some time and know that they fought on *our* side. It was the Germans who tried to destroy you, not the Russians. You are free now. It is over! You can relax! The people of Poland have been liberated."

"Let's go. It is hopeless to talk with the American *Unintelligence* Service!" Johnny rages.

Angry, bewildered, I realize that not only were we forsaken at Yalta, but what is worse, it was done in good will. Their complete lack of accurate information leaves only one solution: self-reliance. In ten years the Americans will understand, but that will be of no help to us, since long before they change their minds about the Russian "friendship," this friendship will bury many of us in Siberian concentration camps.

■ ■ ■

Last night, again, Johnny begged me to go with him to New Zealand. He doesn't understand. I told him I couldn't, that I was committed to help with two more transports. We arrived at the army depot an hour ago and have been sitting in silence at the coffee shop ever since.

I will never marry Johnny. We have been lovers, but I am not in love with him. We are friends; he is one of the best friends I have ever had. For me it is goodbye. I will miss his concern for me and making love with him, but I don't want to be married, tied down. I want to be free; more than anything else, free. I also know there will be other men, for I look and watch. Quietly sipping coffee, saying nothing about a future, perhaps he knows too.

A call comes for his transport to leave, and I walk outside with him, pushed by tears. Johnny grabs me, holds me close against him. I take off a diminutive silver horseshoe pin and give it to him as a *porte-bonheur*, a good-luck charm. He pins it to his shirt.

Johnny jumps on the back of the truck, turns, and waves through the cloud of dust. The dust settles. I will never see Johnny again; that is sad, but I am free.

═ ATOMIC BOMB CAUSES SHOCK ═
AT PAPAL SEE

*Vatican Newspaper Calls it 'Catastrophic,' Tells
Wish That Discoverers Had Destroyed It*

VATICAN CITY (AP)—The Vatican City newspaper L'Osservatore Romano Tuesday called the new atomic bomb "a catastrophic conclusion . . . to the war's apocalyptic surprises."

It compared the invention of the atomic bomb with the invention of a submarine by Leonardo da Vinci, sixteenth century Italian artist and inventor. It expressed regret that the bomb's inventors did not, like da Vinci, destroy their creation in the interest of humanity.

"Da Vinci wanted to defeat death by thought," L'Osservatore said, "but the road of men who have not his Christian charity must defeat death with death. This incredible destructive instrument remains a temptation, if not for horrified contemporaries, then for posterity, to whom little is taught by history."

Msgr. Enrico Pucci's Vatican Press bulletin said that the revelation of the development of the atomic bomb "made a deep impression in the Vatican, not so much for the use already made of the new death instrument as for the sinister shadow that the discovery of this weapon casts on the future of humanity."

LONDON—London predicted the Allies would hand Japan a new ultimatum packing the power of the atomic bomb that blasted Hiroshima. Emperor Hirohito's advisors would have a choice between unconditional surren-

der within 48 hours or oblivion for their sacred
islands, London reports said.

The Milwaukee Journal, *August 7, 1945*

LATE JUNE TO AUGUST 1945

"If I had been there I would have killed the bastard."

While Henri wails with typical French drama, I am
the one who nearly got killed. We argued vehemently
on the way back from Prague. Henri suggested we play
poker.

"Henri, I can only play with American cigarettes or
candy bars. I have no money."

"Save your treasures. Here is some money, a present
. . . and besides, I am going to win it all back from you!"

"Where did you get all that? It's a fortune! You just
gave me ninety dollars."

"I have more," he says, preening like a peacock. "I
did some business with American friends: Borrowed a
car, filled it with Red Cross food and cigarettes, and
took it to Prague; sold it, car included, to the Czechs
and Russians; bought Czech jewelry, then returned to
Pilsen and sold it to the Americans for American cash."

"It's dishonest! Steal from the Russians and the Germans if you like; they are the enemy, but not the
Americans—"

"*Tu m'emmerdes* [you piss me off] with your Ten
Commandments. Deal the cards and shut up."

"I won't shut up. Your behavior stinks."

"Ta gueule!" (Shut up!)

The incident that inspired this conversation began when we arrived at Katowice. Henri bounded off the train to "keep a date," and as I stepped off the train by myself, a group of Russians, fighting among themselves, barred the way. One of the drunks ran after me and grabbed my shoulder, ripping my coat. I swung around and tried to kick him in the groin but missed. Wild with fury, he threw me to the ground, stabbed me in the left side of my back with his bayonet.

When I regained consciousness I was in our railroad ambulatory. Apparently I yelled for help, and when it came, got up and walked. Mrs. Piotrowski washed and bandaged the wound, saying it looked serious and that we would see a doctor first thing in the morning. She gave me a heavy dose of codeine and I slept. This morning I could not straighten up.

Before I finished breakfast, Henri came, like a hurricane, with the news that the next transport was about to leave; only two hours and I must go. It was then that I told him about last night's injury and the wailing began.

Mrs. Piotrowski reiterates over and over that I cannot accompany the transport this time.

"She has a three-inch cut by her kidney. She must see a doctor and she must stay in bed."

"Madame, there is no one else. Ella is in Krakow and there is no time to reach her. The Resistance arranged this transport, during our absence, to include high-ranking Polish underground officers who must be gotten out of this country *now*!"

"But she is ill. You should see the cut. Her kidney—"

"Madame, there is no time to lose. We need her. Christine?"

Knowing Henri well, I am aware this is not one of his games. Groggy most of the time, I see the trip to Prague in a blur as I travel in and out of a codeine haze. By the time we arrive, the wound is badly infected and the location of the pain indicates damage to the kidney as well. There is no possibility of my continuing to Pilsen, so Henri arranges for Count Schönborn to take me to his villa, where a doctor removes the bandages, for the first time in five days. They are crawling with maggots and my stomach revolts at the notion of being eaten alive by worms.

"Christine, it is a good thing they are there, for they have helped control the infection. I am afraid, however, that there is considerable damage to your kidney as well," the doctor says empathetically.

Furious, bitter, frustrated, I rail at "liberation"—the right to be beaten, raped, eaten by maggots. I curse the Red liberators who have nearly killed me.

For several days I lie in a huge bed, gazing out the window over the rooftops of Prague. The velvet draperies undulate in the wind and the dark oriental rugs feel soft on my feet when I briefly stand. The food is exquisite, the roses on my nightstand are replaced daily, and the door is always left a bit ajar so that I might hear the count playing on the grand piano in the library.

"Christine, the wound is much better, healing nicely." The doctor beams at the rapidity of my recovery.

"It is impossible not to feel better in this house," I reply. "I could stay forever."

Forever is ten days. His business ventures in Pilsen completed, Henri takes me to the train for Poland.

It is a dark, rainy night as the train stops in Katowice. Henri insists that this time he will accompany me all the way home. As we pass the first-aid center we see a dim light, so we enter, hoping that Ella will be back from Krakow and on duty. Mary, another nurse, stiffens and seems to catch her breath, as if frightened and trying to warn me. Before she can utter a word, Andrejew emerges from the shadows to greet me.

"You must come with me."

"Where to?"

"To my office."

"What's the matter, Andrejew?"

"Oh, it is nothing, *niczywo;* only a few questions the NKVD want to ask you. They ordered me to deliver you to their office as soon as I see you. Come on, let's go!"

I feel terror, try to appear unconcerned.

"Andrejew, if it is just *niczywo,* why don't we go tomorrow? It is so late and I am exhausted from my trip. My side isn't healed, you know."

Unable to understand our Polish, Henri yanks my arm, knowing that something critical is taking place.

"Henri, he insists that he must take me to the NKVD for questioning," I tell him in French.

Henri visibly trembles. Andrejew ignores both of us, then takes my arm, not gently, but like huge tongs holding on to a log, and pushes me outside into his car.

We speed along the dark streets to Katowice Prison,

where the NKVD has its office. Andrejew is friendly as he helps me out of the car, yet he knows very well what bringing me to the NKVD signifies.

"Andrejew, please! Let me go. My side hurts and I need to go home. This can wait."

The begging repulses me, but I am desperate. Andrejew takes my arm and walks me into the building. There a Russian policeman sitting behind a desk smiles at him, a smile I cannot interpret. Andrejew orders me to give the policeman my I.D., pats me on the shoulder, and utters two words: *"Do swidania."* (Goodbye.)

Now it is the policeman who orders me to follow him down a long dirty corridor to an empty room.

"Wait here."

Stop shaking and think, I say to myself when the door opens and a middle-aged man, rather nice-looking, enters.

"Is your name Wieczorek?"

"Yes," I answer, wondering if he knows my real name.

"As a convoy nurse, how many times have you been to Pilsen? Was it twice or three times? And what can you tell me about the smuggling of reactionary elements?"

I study his face. He is so blunt, so to the point. He didn't ask a lot of questions leading up to the important one, but just spat it out. I must calculate my response carefully. The acute pain disappears as the adrenaline of fear takes over. I stare at him without flinching.

"I was in Pilsen once. I have escorted transports to Prague and have no idea what you mean by 'smuggling reactionaries'?"

"So, you have no idea? Perhaps you have forgotten? Would you like me to remind you?" He growls angrily.

"All I know is that the Russian authorities ordered me to assist the sick refugees and gave me permission to travel from Poland to Czechoslovakia. If I had wanted to run away from Poland I could have easily done so."

"I am not asking if you wanted to run away," he barks. "I am not interested in you at all. I want to know who went west on those transports other than the authorized refugees."

"I told you, I don't know. I only saw refugees."

"All right, have your way."

He summons a warden, who grabs me roughly by the shoulder and forces me down a long corridor toward a steep staircase that leads to the cellar. He shoves me down the stairs, unlocks the door, and pushes me inside. Stumbling down a few more steps, I manage not to fall. The door slams behind me and I am left in total darkness, standing in water an inch above my ankles. It is very quiet, yet in spite of the silence, I know I am not alone. There is the nauseating stench of rotten flesh and excrement. It is an Auschwitz odor. To keep from vomiting, I light one of the American cigarettes still in my pocket. The match goes out as I light the tip of my cigarette, and I have no time to see anything. Water now splashes from all sides.

"Who is that?"

Only silence.

"Who is that?"

My voice, louder and more determined, echoes back to me, intensifying my fear.

"Prisoners!" a growling voice answers, and a hand snatches away my cigarette.

"You needn't steal. I have cigarettes and will give you some with pleasure. How many of you are there?"

A different voice answers.

"With you, eleven alive and two dead. They died a few days ago and no one has come to remove them, so we put them one on top of another to make us a seat."

"A stinking bench," adds a third voice.

I cannot believe it; cold fear has gripped me, and I am unable to move. I am going to be sick.

"Where is the toilet?"

"No toilet, just shit where you are."

"Oh, Jesus Christ."

I call out loud. My cigarettes given away, a few wavering flames from the matches do not pierce the darkness, but the smoke helps to ease the stench. Someone approaches me, touches my shoulder. I scream. "What do you want?"

"Calm down, I won't hurt you. In the morning we have a little light here from the windows. You will see our place then. We are all political prisoners, left here to be finished off. They only keep us alive because they want us to reveal the names of others. I tell you, it *is* hell."

My mind churns with questions I dare not ask; the answers would intensify my fears.

"Don't stand in one place. Move about. This place is full of rats, and if one of them bites you, you will die of blood poisoning."

All through the rest of the night I follow his advice,

hanging on to the wall for support, trying not to think, concentrating on where I am going and what I am stepping on. I mustn't fall. The night is full of noises. Each step amplifies the motion of the water. One prisoner finally falls asleep, his snoring causing reverberations in the walls and water. Desperate for sleep, aching all over, I dare not stop moving.

The first ray of sunligh intrudes through a pane of glass, rubbed clean in the shape of a cross by one of the prisoners. There is nothing left and faith is all I have to hold on to. Staring at the little cross, I try to pray, can find no words. Beyond, there is fresh air and freedom. I am on the wrong side of the cross.

When I turn around to examine the cellar, shapes begin to emerge. One man sits on top of a barrel, another on the end of a beam sticking out of the water. They resemble monkeys perched in a zoo. Others are standing or leaning against the wall. Why don't they move? Their feet will rot off in this stinking water or be consumed by rats.

In one corner two men sit on something I cannot quite make out in the dim light, and next to them a third person is half sitting, half lying with his head propped against a water pipe. *No!* Oh, my God, it's not a man . . . it's a girl—wearing a nurse's uniform. No, it cannot be. It's just some nurse from somewhere, but not one of us. Her left arm hangs limp with a bracelet I recognize at once. It is Ella's.

I turn away in order not to see her and have the truth confirmed. I appeal to the little cross in the window.

"God, please, not her, let it be someone else, another girl with the same bracelet, in the same uniform, but please, God, not Ella." Motionless, trying to gain time, hoping to find the courage to face truth, I finally take a step toward her, leaving the frightened part of me at the cross, the other part trying to be brave.

Miracles do not happen. There is no doubt. Ella. Her face, swollen and bruised, is battered almost beyond recognition. Her eyes do not open as I take her arms and try to pull her upright. Oh, my God, Jesus, Mary! She is sitting on two bodies, on what was once a human face, now all distorted and rotten, staring at me. A scream chokes in my throat as I drop Ella back the way she was. Her expression does not change. The man sitting next to her asks, "Did you know her? They took her for questioning the other day and that is how she returned. They have smashed her skull. Don't waste your strength helping her, she is as good as dead."

I do not answer him. I want to go back to the cross and curse it but am stopped by a small group standing there, singing with their feeble voices, their hands folded in morning prayer. They have so much more than I have, with my hate, rebellion, cursing. I join them and begin to sing, having no idea why. At first a whisper, then an open note of song; as I sing with the others an extraordinary feeling passes through me, one of belonging. I am not alone anymore. These people, these cursed and damned people, are my friends.

When the prayers and singing are finished, I turn to the only other woman and ask, "Do they ever feed you?"

"Oh yes, they give us a pail of soup each day. It is water and cabbage, and not much of it at that, but we share it and it does keep us alive."

Most of us are moving again, like a merry-go-round, in circles. I look back to the corner against the wall for Ella. She is no longer there; the two men are sitting on a higher bench.

Three days pass, all alike. Several more have died, some because of their beatings, others, as the grim joke goes among us, of natural causes; starvation, heart attack, disease. There are six of us left.

No one has beaten me and my side hurts less. I am overrun with lice, scratch all the time, but feel lucky, as I have had the inoculation for spotted fever and there is little chance these lice will give me the disease.

"Say, how about a game of cards? You could win millions!" I suggest, pulling out a deck from my pocket.

"Yes! Why not? Let's play," the voices respond.

We rearrange the bodies, covering them with boards found on the floor under the water, then sit in a circle using our knees as tables. As we begin to play, the pale, swaying young woman, the one I first asked about food, flops down, leaning against my shoulder, and in a voice so weak I can barely hear her, questions, "Can I play with you?"

They questioned her yesterday and her face is a mess, eyes half open and dried blood all around her broken nose. The beatings did not cause severe injuries to the rest of her body, but both of her legs are black from gangrene. She must have had wounds on her feet, and the filthy water has done its work. As she leans against me I feel her burning fever and hope, for her, that she will die quickly.

We play for absurdly high stakes, to be paid after we are released and are free—a dream as real as the millions we bet and lose in a few moments. Hush! There are footsteps on the stairs; keep playing, pretend the descending feet will move in another direction. The door opens, a name shouted.

"Wieczorek!"

Then called again louder.

"Wieczorek!"

I wonder which one of us he is calling. Jolted, I realize it is the name I used on my forged pass. As I move the woman next to me from my shoulder to another's, I imagine myself in the same state. I don't want to leave my cellar jail; it is safer here than upstairs. The name is shouted again, so I stumble toward the door. There are two wardens this time, one of whom has great difficulty, as he is intoxicated and about to pass out. Placed in the same room as before, with the same NKVD interrogator, I struggle for composure.

"Well, have you had enough of it? Are you ready to tell the truth now? If you do, you can leave through this door, a free person."

"No, I can tell you nothing more now than I told you before. That is the truth. It is all I know."

His face remains rocklike as he stands and with full

strength belts my face with the back of his hand. My nose gushes with blood, reverberations bounce off the back of my head. I wipe the blood with my sleeve.

"Will you talk now?"

"No, I cannot tell you anything more."

He rises again, moves toward me, raises his arm, and stops as another man in civilian clothes enters. They consult in words I do not recognize, then abruptly turn and call the warden to return me to my cell. All of the old prisoners are gone, including the dead ones. There are many new ones chatting, in comparison full of hope. There is no one to tell them the truth except me, and I am not about to tell anything. I sit on the barrel, head in my hands, a loud buzzing in my ears. I can no longer hold back the tears.

The sun is gone and the fading light is so dim that even the little cross doesn't show anymore. In the darkness I hear feet coming down those stairs again. The drunk warden opens the door, calls my name. I get off the barrel and trudge toward him. It doesn't matter anymore. The only feelings that matter are the loss of my prison friends with whom I have spent these terrible long days.

The warden, more drunk than before, grabs my arm twice to steady himself as we return to the room for interrogation. This time a new man fires questions at me, and with each "I don't know" he hits me harder and harder, until in a final rage he throws me to the floor and kicks at me. The room spins, gets hazy, disappears.

■ ■ ■

A glass of water has just been poured on my face. It is difficult to open my swollen eyes and the whole room is a moving blur. Apparently the interrogator has left and only the drunk warden remains. He pulls me brutally to my feet, grabbing my arms so that I scream with pain. My side, stabbed at the station in Katowice, feels like it has ripped apart, while my face burns and stings, with sharp jabs throbbing through my head.

I am dazed, arms hanging like leaden weights, as the warden pushes me out of the room, mumbling that we are going back to the cell. He turns in the wrong direction, moving me toward another section of the prison. I am so confused that I call his attention to the mistake. With a *"niet"* and a thunderous belch, he opens the door and shoves me into a different cell on the first floor.

I don't want to be here. As horrible as it was, I want to be back in the room with the little cross. I know that room in spite of its horror; I have gotten used to it, know what to do there. I try to examine the new room, but my eyes see only shadows through slits in the swelling. It seems a large place, like an unfurnished hall, with no bars and a sink on one wall. The room is too bright, the light too painful, so I close my swollen eyes tight.

I don't have the strength to jerk back when I feel someone touch me. Someone is caressing my head and whispering, "Countess, what have they done to you?"

I can't believe what I am hearing. I am sure the beatings have made me delirious and that I am imagining things. Again I hear, "Countess, please. It is I. Please look at me."

Slowly I open my eyes, struggle to focus, and still can't believe, certain it is a dream. Zofia, the prostitute from the transport who was so good about helping to pass out food and taking care of the children, touches me very gently and smiles when I finally show that I recognize her. She looks as if her heart would break.

"Such a disgrace for you, being here among us. We are all whores in this room."

Weakly I press my hand against her mouth and whisper, "Shush, Zofia. Please do not call me Countess and do not use my name. Call me Wieczorek."

She helps me to my feet; straightening my arms and legs sends pain through my back and shoulders. Allowing me to use her as a crutch, she manages to help me hobble to the sink. As we cross the room, through the slits of my swollen eyes I see the other girls, the inmates, all street women. I question Zofia.

"Why are you all here?"

"Oh, mostly for being on the streets after curfew. Nothing serious. They will let all of us out tomorrow morning. I have been here many times before."

Unembarrassed, I strip off all of my clothes in front of everyone and start to wash, both myself and my clothes. The soap, liquid, dark, and rough, is too strong even to wash a kitchen floor, but no kitchen floor is as dirty as I am. I put the clothes back on wet and feel better. Talking with Zofia, I stare straight into her eyes and decide that I will tell her everything so that she will know the full extent of the danger, should she choose to help me escape. Opening up this way to her does not feel like much of a risk, as Zofia has a large heart and there is little to lose. There is no one else to help; her response is quick and spontaneous.

"Countess, often toward early morning the Russians coming off duty come here to help themselves to a girl. I have my makeup kit with me, so we can use powder, rouge, and cover-up cream. The bruises will be hidden, then I know how to fix your hair. It will give you a chance to be picked up by a soldier, especially one who is drunk. They all have rooms out of town, so if you are picked up you know what to do."

"Zofia, what are you saying?"

"Fight for your life any way you can, even if you have to become one of us for a moment. You *have* slept with a man, haven't you?"

I smile. It sounds so ironic, taking lessons from a whore; yet she is instructing me in life's most important subject: how to survive.

Zofia worked on my face and hair a good part of the night. With clean dry clothes and heavy rouge on my swollen lips, I look like a different person.

"Countess, let's move to the front so that you will be the first to be noticed. Here, take some of my perfume. These Russians love it."

She opens her cheap bottle of perfume and pours it all over me. It is reminiscent of the night in Warsaw when I poured the bottle of perfume on my hair to impress Tatek. I wonder if once again I smell like "dogs who have rolled in dead fish." Zofia has returned from one of the other girls with several strings of beads.

"Here, put these on to help cover the black and blue marks on your neck. The bastard must have grabbed you by the throat. There, Countess, you look good in beads."

We move to the front of the room near the door and sit on the floor. Zofia leaves again, returning minutes later with a piece of bread and butter. It is the first solid food I have eaten since I was arrested. It tastes good, but my throat is so sore that I have trouble swallowing. To be so hungry and to have it hurt so much . . . I cannot eat it all.

The door opens and a Russian soldier walks in. He looks around, his eyes stopping as they catch mine. He smiles, but I cannot smile back. I hate him. He repulses me. He walks up to another girl, who smiles, then takes her hand and leaves. Zofia is angry.

"What were you waiting for? For God's sake don't miss your chance. You may only have a few of them. You are fighting for your life, so don't be so stupid!"

She takes my hand in both of hers, caressing it gently, her eyes pleading.

"Countess, please, do not refuse the next one. Go and do what he wants, then run like hell. Once you are free, come to my place."

Her address is a small attic room in one of the outlying sections of Katowice.

"You will be safe there with me. I will contact Mr. Henri and then he can help to get you out of Poland."

"Oh, Zofia, I thank you and I will try the next time. I will try to do what you want me to do."

We sit in silence and wait. Maybe there won't be a

second chance. I feel degraded, but why should I feel that way? It is stupid. I have a choice, maybe, between going to bed with a Russian and buying freedom or returning to the watery cellar cell, a certain grave. Do I or do I not want to live? Of course I want to live. Yes, yes, and once more yes, at any price. So why do I hesitate?

Will there be a next time? Can I really go through with it? I can. I can do anything if I put my mind to it. But it is all so repulsive and beyond dignity. I won't think about it. I will think only about the cell and the benches made out of dead bodies, of Ella, of the stench and the beatings. Yes, that is what I will think about.

I am so deep in thought, I do not notice another Russian soldier at the door. Zofia nudges me. I look at him with a forced smile. I will pay this price for freedom. He takes my hand as I get up from the floor. The last thing I hear is a whisper from Zofia.

"Szczęść Boże." (God speed.)

=== **PEACE!** ===

THE JAPS GIVE UP UNCONDITIONALLY—
ALLIED TROOPS TOLD TO CEASE FIRING;
ENEMY GETS ORDERS FOR SURRENDER

THE POTSDAM DECLARATION ACCEPTED,
TRUMAN DECLARES IN AN
OFFICIAL STATEMENT

WASHINGTON, AUG. 14—Peace came to the world tonight when President Truman an-

nounced that Japan has accepted unconditional surrender and that Allied forces have
been ordered to cease firing.

General Douglas MacArthur, "the man
who came back," was named Supreme Allied
Commander to receive the formal Japanese
Surrender.

World War II—the bloodiest conflict in
human history—was at an end, except for the
formality of signing surrender documents.

V-J day will not be proclaimed until after
the instruments of surrender are signed.

America's three allies—Great Britain, Russia and China—will be represented at the
signing by high ranking officers.

San Francisco Chronicle, August 15, 1945

EARLY SEPTEMBER 1945

For a split second I feel compassion for this animal, this
Russian, more ape than human. I do not hate him but
want to thank him for what he has done, for setting me
free. Without a rustle I get up while he sleeps. There
are vodka bottles on the floor, vomit over the tables and
chairs, reminders which quickly erase the compassion.
He is horrible, more so because of the price I paid for
last night's freedom.

The Russian ripped off my clothes, threw me on the
bed, and attacked like a starving animal. Too drunk to

notice the bruises or react to my groans, he took his pleasure as he ravaged my body. It was a defilement.

I noiselessly leave the room and start running. Strength surges in me and I run faster. Finally, in a small village outside Katowice, I stop running and lie down near a thicket of willows along the edge of a brook. Hidden from the rest of the world, I collapse in a deep sleep uninterrupted by dreams or nightmares. I sense the warmth of the noonday sun, stretch a bit, and sleep on. Sometime as the night air grows colder I pull my clothing more tightly around me. The cool air of early fall cannot pierce my need for sleep, the fatigue that has invaded every inch of my physical being and my spirit. It is not until the next morning that I awaken. I am so cold I can barely move.

I need to find Zofia's place on the other side of Katowice. I hitch several short rides, skirting the dangers of the city center. As Zofia opens the door to her attic room, her face is a sunburst of joy.

"Thank God you are here. Come in!"

I try to account for what happened, but she puts me off, insisting that we eat first.

"Sit down, Countess, sit down. Everything is almost ready. Sit down, I will bring it."

There is potato soup with bits of bacon and other vegetables, bread, real butter, and coffee that tastes like coffee. I wonder where she found it but do not ask. Every taste deserves savoring. Zofia is pleased.

She darts into her closet and comes out with a new set of clothes.

"Here, try these on, they ought to fit you. I got them

from a friend who is about your height . . . and you will want to wash . . . I'll heat water. You can go behind the screen. There is a basin, soap, and towels for you."

Now she is busy making a bed for me. I marvel at this woman, so different from me, yet so kind and gentle, so concerned about my well-being. I glance at a mirror behind the screen but turn away, saying to myself, "No! I will look at Christine a week from now. Tonight I look as if I had been taken off the church at Notre Dame, a gargoyle."

Washed and dressed, I emerge from behind the screen to find Zofia ready for her business of the evening. Her cheeks are highly colored and her lips stretch in both directions. Her eye shadow is deep and her lashes long and darkened.

"Countess, I will have to leave in a moment. My customers will be here, and they don't like to wait. Make yourself comfortable and don't worry. There is an apple cheese in the cupboard and it is very good. Help yourself."

The stillness of the night is interrupted by the noisy continuous blowing of a horn. The offending car is below the window. The door closes and I pull aside the window curtains to see below. Startled at first, I relax as I watch Zofia join the Russian soldier and the two other girls in the command car below. A shiver goes through me as they race off into the night.

Lying on my freshly made bed, I think about Zofia and the life she leads. She considers herself to be repulsive, outcast, bad. That is a shame. She is one of the most honest, the most caring people I have ever met.

Life's ironic paradoxes infiltrate my dreams as I fall asleep.

His screaming echoes up the stairwell. At first a dream, then recognition; of course, the voice is Henri's. He cries, embraces me, almost choking me, while speaking so fast I cannot understand all that he says. Between *chérie* and *merde* there is an ocean of joy with incoherent words. Finally, out of breath, he quits.

Zofia is here, too, smiling as she prepares breakfast for the three of us. A swallow of warm coffee, and Henri continues.

"You know I spent all of my money trying to get you out, but I didn't know where you were. Andrejew promised, after four cases of vodka and two watches, to find out about you and arrange your release. He said you would be released in a day or—"

I interrupt. "Henri, no one got out alive from that hell. Ella was there; she died!"

"Oh, *mon Dieu*," Henri whispers, his eyes filling with tears. He sits motionless, struck dumb by what I have just told him. Henri never weeps and his tears make me wonder, for I am not sure he liked Ella, except for the fact that she was my friend.

I am drained of all emotion.

I have been at Zofia's for a week now, enjoying her mothering and continual attention. The communication between us is open and intense. She asks me to tell her in as much detail as possible what happened between the Russian and myself, not out of curiosity, but because of an innate understanding that it would help me, that the telling might take away some of the numbness and the pain. When I hesitate, she prods.

"And when he threw you on the bed?"

I recount how I continually thought of something other than what I was doing: of Ella and her beaten face; of the train ride in 1939 when the criminal said he had killed my parents; of the doll graveyard at Adampol where in my mind I buried him forever.

"Countess, did he make you do things that hurt you?" Zofia's tone is so gentle.

"Zofia, he made me do things that I cannot tell you. They were too revolting, too disgusting. My greatest fear is pregnancy or disease."

"Yes, we must do something about that now."

We put on our coats and without appointment see a friend of hers, a doctor who assures me there is no sign of venereal disease but adds, "Too soon to know about pregnancy."

I inform Zofia that if I am pregnant I will have an abortion. I will not give birth to that Russian's child, as I would hate it as much as him. I know it is illegal, against the teachings of my church, my family, but I *will* have one.

Henri visits me every day, keeping me informed about the next transport, through Prague in the Russian zone, to Pilsen in the American zone. We have all agreed that I will join it as a passenger, the wife of a Frenchman, blond, pregnant. It is such irony. Henri arranges the necessary papers and Zofia rearranges my appearance.

My hair is dyed straw yellow, a large pillow is laced around my stomach, and other cosmetic changes make me look like an eight-month-pregnant expectant mother. To check the authenticity of the disguise, Henri sends Mary, the nurse at the first aid center the night of my arrest, to see me. When I answer the door, she asks, as if I were an utter stranger, "I have come to see Christine. Is she here?"

Henri arrives in a "borrowed" car to drive me to a station some miles from Katowice, where I will board the westbound train. It is time to leave Zofia's attic. I have become so attached to this street woman.

"Zofia, thank you."

My shaky voice reveals the emotion I feel for her. She knows it, moves toward me, and stops, hesitating, not knowing what to do. To her, the distance between countess and whore remains painful, so far and yet so close. I reach forward and hug her. She kisses my blond hair, pats my cheek.

"Countess, it has been such an honor for me."

In my heart there is no distance. I owe her my life.

Silently, I ride in the car with Henri, wondering about the precautions we have taken. Are they necessary? I am probably forgotten, assumed dead in the stinking water of the Katowice prison cellar. The NKVD has a surplus of suspects for questioning; hundreds of more important people have been arrested. But I don't blame myself for being afraid. Fear, these last months, has become an obsession.

The convoy is small, mostly men, only four women, about fifty in all. I climb aboard the train and enter the compartment with the other women. They are all, like myself, escaping the country. This time, the procedure having become a bit obvious, Henri has decided against vodka and prostitutes. Replaced by the NKVD, who are not such easy prey to alcohol and women, fewer Russian soldiers patrol the border. With errorless forged passports and a small group of people who speak several languages, ours seems a safe plan.

Civilian border officials enter the train to check our papers. One opens our compartment door, asks for our papers, and orders us to leave the train and go to the station office. I don't like it. We look at each other, the four of us silent, tense with thoughts and questions for which we have no answers. Once in the station we are escorted to a back room, where we are told to undress; our clothes will be searched.

Terror afflicts me. The first woman recedes behind the screen, hangs her clothes on the edge of it, and calls the woman inspector when fully undressed. The second does exactly the same. Now it is my turn.

Trapped again, I marvel at the stupidity of my disguise. I am a bony skeleton, five feet eight, weighing barely ninety pounds, with a pillow on my stomach. A frightful sense of hopelessness pervades. The policewoman, obviously, has noted my pregnancy. I must now take off everything and stand naked in my deception. I put the pillow on the chair, sit on it, and with a shaky voice manage to call the policewoman. She enters, stares at me from head to toe, and examines each piece of clothing. Her face reveals neither feeling nor thought. She is meticulous in her search. Please get it over with and call

the guards, or do you get sadistic joy out of the interminable delay? Suddenly she smiles!

"That's fine. I have seen enough. You may get dressed
and go back to the train."

Stunned, I blink and she is gone. Why? Is she stupid?
Kind? On our side? With utmost speed I dress, stick the
pillow back in place, and return to the train. The woman
. . . ? More questions never answered.

We arrive in Prague after dusk. I decide not to leave
the station except to take the first train going to the
American zone. The wait will be less than an hour. Now
I must say goodbye to Henri.

He has been good to me, has never made passes the
many times we were on the train together. Looking at
him now, I understand that in his own way, he cared
for me and respected me. However, leaving is not sad.
When the train comes, I board. Henri says *"bonne
chance"* and cautions me to be careful. I wave to him,
then look in another direction.

There is one more border to cross, one more Russian
investigation. No, I cannot endure that trauma, so I will
get off the train just before the border station and cross
on foot from the Russian to the American zone. Passing
through woods and fields my chances are good, as the
night is dark and the Russian patrols stay close to town.

I stand now, ready to jump. The train slows on a curve
just before entering the town. Next to the tracks there
are bushes, but it is too dark to see anything else. On
the steps at the exit end of the car, I try to remember
what Henri told me about the technique of jumping off
a train. I can't remember. Do you jump with or against

the direction of the train? The thought scares me and my not remembering frightens me even more, as he once explained that if I jumped in the wrong direction I could be pulled under the wheels of the train.

Time has run out. I can guess no longer. Hoping the landing will not be too rough, I jump straight ahead, as far as I can.

I am in midair, falling toward the ground. The train moves on.

═══ RUSSIA ═══

The Conquerors

The rain poured down on Marshal Joseph Stalin and his commissars as they stood atop Lenin's red granite mausoleum. It poured down on 200 unblinking Red Army soldiers as they marched stiff-legged across Moscow's Red Square. It drenched the 1,400 piece military band and the cheering crowds who braved the weather to see Marshal Konstantin Rokossovsky (on a black horse) and Marshal Georgi Zhukov (on a white horse) lead rumbling masses of tanks and motorized artillery in Russia's biggest victory celebration.

But most of the eyes were on the 200 soldiers. Each of them carried a captured German flag bedecked with captured German medals. Suddenly the massed band stopped blaring. Only hundreds of drums rumbled. As the 200 soldiers approached Lenin's tomb they lowered the German flags (including Hitler's personal standard) and dragged them over the muddy cobblestones. In front of Lenin's tomb the soldiers, without turning their heads or breaking step, tossed the flags into the mud.

There were special victory awards to Marshal Stalin too. By decree of the Supreme Soviet he became the second living European to receive the title of Generalissimo (the first; Generalissimo Francisco Franco). Generalissimo Stalin was also awarded the Order of Victory, the Gold Star Medal of Hero of the Soviet Union, and the Order of Lenin.

Time, *July 9, 1945*

Part Four

THE
AMERICAN

Get up! Get up! You're going home! Roll out of that sack and cram your stuff into your barracks bags and swing 'em on that truck waiting out front. You're going where houses are built the way you like to see them, and where the streetlamps go on at night and where a macadam road winds around the corner and its tar grows hot and sticky in summer and trees lean over and cool it by breathing softly. You're going to a place where lights go on when you push a button and hot meals are served in china plates and clean water runs at the twist of your wrist and starched shirts come out of a paper package and you can sit on a toilet seat in privacy, and walk erect without fear and say good night to friends and know that you will see them alive some other time, and take your wife in your arms without a schedule of train departures in your hip pocket. . . .

Life is a magnificent purse of gold thrown in people's laps, and all they have brains to hold onto is a bent penny. . . .

People don't know how to live. They only have suspicions.

from *Beach Red*
by Peter Bowman, 1945

THE AMERICAN

My knees hit the ground, scraping rock, dirt, and grass. I can feel how deeply I have skinned them and they hurt terribly. I touch my legs and feel the blood gushing down. I have to sit for a while, but as time passes the pain begins to subside. My eyes become accustomed to the dark, and now I can see, just a few yards away, a small pond, its surface lit by the moon. Slowly I move toward it and put my legs into the cool water. At first the burning pain is awful and I bite my lips to keep from screaming, but gradually it eases and I am able to get up and start walking.

I have to avoid villages, yet follow the direction of the railroad tracks so as not to lose my way. Far ahead I can see the dim lights of the border station, so I circle it, walking on the outskirts of the town. It is only a couple of miles, but it takes me a long time; I keep stumbling on tree stumps and must thrash my way through branches. "I have to stand, to walk, if I am to reach the Allied zone before daylight," I say to myself.

After what seems an endless journey, I reach the top of a small hill. From there I can see the dim lights of the Russian border town well behind me.

Now I know that all dangers have been passed, so I go back to the railroad tracks and follow them to the next station. The station building is well lit, and on it I can see the American flag.

In a daze I walk up to the platform and sit down on a bench, waiting for the next train to Pilsen. The darkness of the night is slowly changing to the grays of the morning, with the sun on the horizon. I know the nightmare is over, and that what I fought for and suffered so much for is now mine: my life.

The roar of a jeep driving up to the station startles me. The driver, an American lieutenant in a khaki Eisenhower jacket, approaches me, grinning. He is young, my age.

"Oh, you had a bad fall. You should take care of those knees of yours."

I don't want to talk about my knees—but I answer, "It is nothing, a little scrape. They will heal soon."

"Are you waiting for the train to Pilsen? I'm driving there. Give you a lift if you want."

"Thank you, yes."

I get up and walk with him to his jeep.

"Hop in," he says.

As we start to drive off, I look back and whisper to myself, "God, please protect the ones I left behind, the ones I love, the ones I will always remember."

"Did you say something?" the lieutenant asks.

"No, not really, nothing important."

The lieutenant examines my knees again.

"Hey, you've had a rough time . . . with your boyfriend? . . . Too much booze? . . . It wasn't a G.I., was it? You really should take care of those knees."

He grins, an American—buoyant, laughing, flirtatious. "Well, are you going to tell me what kind of trouble you got into last night?"

I look up at his young, uncomprehending face.

"Trouble? Not really," I answer. "Though I guess you could call it maybe just a little bit of trouble."

EPILOGUE

The postwar years brought many turbulent experiences. Although I reached the free West in 1945, I had to continue to struggle for freedom and human dignity until I came to the United States in November 1947, and like any other refugee, tried to build a new life for myself and my husband in a place I could adopt as my new country.

Having lived in the U.S. occupied zone of Germany for two years, I had grown fond of Americans and my dream became to settle down in America. But to achieve this goal I had to cope with the complicated regulations which at that time governed U.S. immigration laws in Germany, and these forced me to marry Julius Panek.

We had met in the American zone in Germany, at Munich, while working together in UNRRA, the United Nations Relief and Rehabilitation Administration. He was twenty years older than I, a judge with a degree in international law who had worked for the Polish Ministry of Foreign Affairs before the war.

He was all the things I hadn't wanted in a husband and I was all the things he hadn't wanted in a wife. But by marrying we gained the required status to obtain a visa to the United States.

"Till divorce do us part" were the vows we took, and we agreed to divorce as soon as we reached America. But we broke our vows and remained married for over twenty years.

When we arrived in New York on the ex-troop transport

the *Marine Tiger,* all the other refugees had people waiting to greet them. But we had no one and only a dollar and fifty cents between us. We had been sent earlier than expected, and our sponsor, to whom my husband had been referred when he was working for the Nuremberg trials, was nowhere to be found.

A cleaner on the docks saw our desperate situation and took pity on us. He said, "I have a friend in the Bowery where you can live for a dollar fifty a week." We walked there, and as soon as we went inside, my husband, more experienced than I, recognized immediately that we were in a house of ill repute.

The man in charge of all the girls there had been in the American army that liberated Dachau, where my husband had been interned. He liked my husband and found me a job cleaning the streets outside a wholesale market. A lot of vegetables were discarded in the gutters; I would bring them home, and that is how we lived. At Christmastime the prostitutes took a collection and gave us a hundred dollars as a Christmas present, and that enabled us to get to Boston, where we wanted to settle down.

There I took any job I could get, eventually became a nurse's aide at the New England Hospital for Women and Children, then passed the civil service examination to become a vocational rehabilitation counselor and worked with the mentally and physically handicapped for twenty years. In 1976 I was chosen Counselor of the Year by the Rehabilitation Commission. In my spare time I lectured on my war experiences. Many of the clubs and organizations that heard me sent food, clothes, and medicine to my family in Poland. Between 1950 and 1955 about twelve people were able to survive thanks only to the generosity of my listeners.

After my husband died, I retired and in 1977 moved to Kennebunk, Maine. I continued to work with the mentally ill at the Webber Hospital in Biddeford.

My biggest achievement in America was to rid myself of all bitterness and hate. I was able to replace these feelings with acceptance and understanding. Devoting my life to working with handicapped people often made me realize how lucky I was, and how little I had to complain about.

I had come here as a nobody. Whether I picked vegetables or cleaned streets, I was always climbing higher. But for my husband, an accomplished person, it was more difficult. He felt degraded, useless. He never really adjusted to our new life.

Eventually my parents and my brother Jerome, cousin Andrew, and sister Basia were all able to leave Poland and settle in the free West.

Jerome escaped from Poland in 1946, the year after I did, and went to South Africa, where Andrew later joined him. My mother and father came to Boston in 1957. My father, who was ill, worked for a time as a guard at the Boston Museum of Fine Arts. He died in 1963. My mother then came to live with me until her death in 1985. She worked as a housekeeper/hostess for the New England Conservatory of Music until she was seventy-eight years old. When she retired they honored her by giving her a professor's chair. I had not heard my younger sister Basia's voice in thirty-five years. Then one day in

1980 the phone rang. She had managed to get a visitor's visa and she was here, in the United States, where she has stayed in Maine.

Now only Basia and Andrew and I are alive. But there were joyful moments when we were all reunited as a family, and those few moments of happiness linger as bright memories.

When my mother died four years ago, I had no desire to stay on in Maine without her. In a newspaper I saw a picture of a small town in Virginia—Scottsville—and I thought, why not move there?

So today, widowed, I live in Scottsville, where I have re-created a small Adampol; I have my dogs, a cottage, and two acres of woods. It is a miniature of what was, yet the same sun that shone on the thousands of acres and the palace shines here giving the same light and warmth, permitting all creatures to live in peace.

Christine Zamoyska-Panek
Scottsville, Virginia
February 1989